The PURPOSE OF THIS BOOK IS TO DISSOLVE THE FEARS OFTEN ASSOCIATED WITH PERSPECTIVE DRAWING —— AND TO FURNISH A WORKING KNOWLEDGE OF THE SUBJECT. ▪ ▪ ▪ ▪ ▪ ▪ ▪

SIMPLE OBJECTS HAVE BEEN CHOSEN AND SIMPLE DIAGRAMS HAVE BEEN USED TO SHOW HOW IT IS DONE AND WHY. ANY PERSON WHO STUDIES THIS BOOK CAREFULLY WILL FIND, TO HIS SURPRISE, THAT IT HAS GIVEN HIM WHAT HE NEEDS TO TURN OUT A GOOD PERSPECTIVE DRAWING.

VERY TRULY YOURS,

Ernest Norling

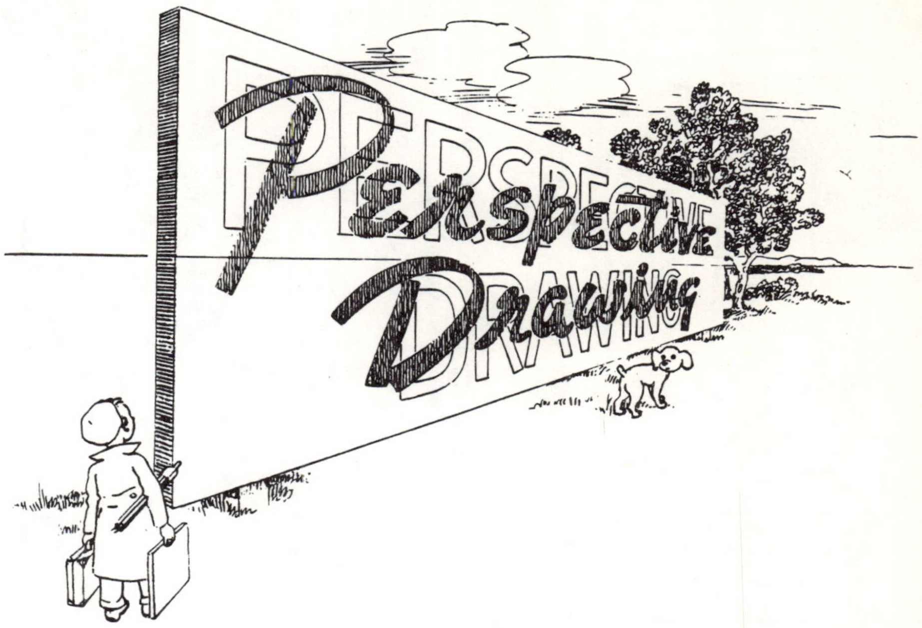

PERSPECTIVE MAKES THE THING WE ARE DRAWING LOOK SOLID.

THE PLAN—THEN THE DRAWING IN DIMENSION.

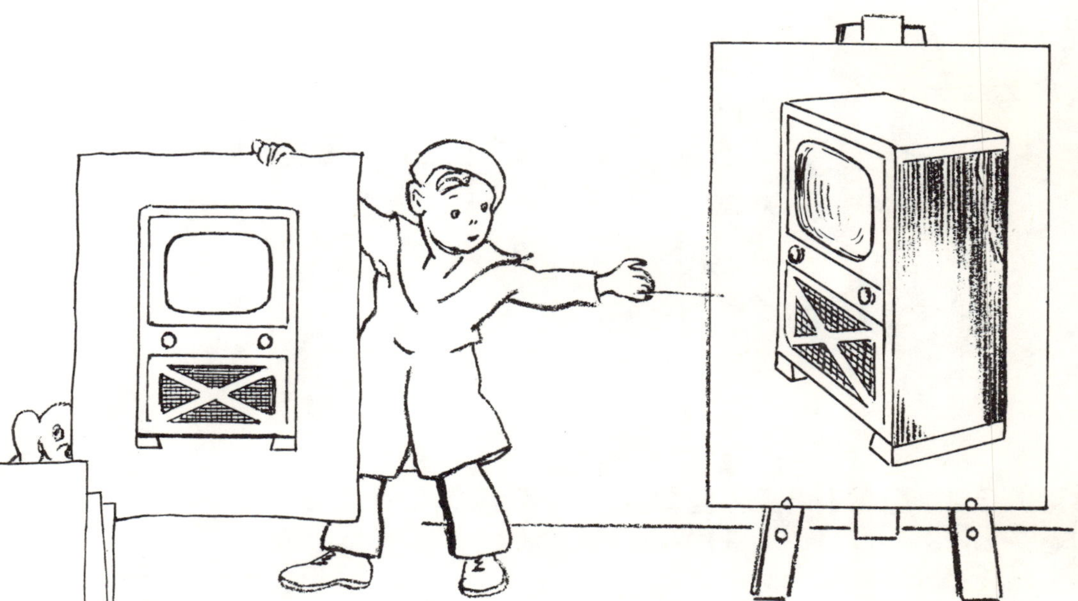

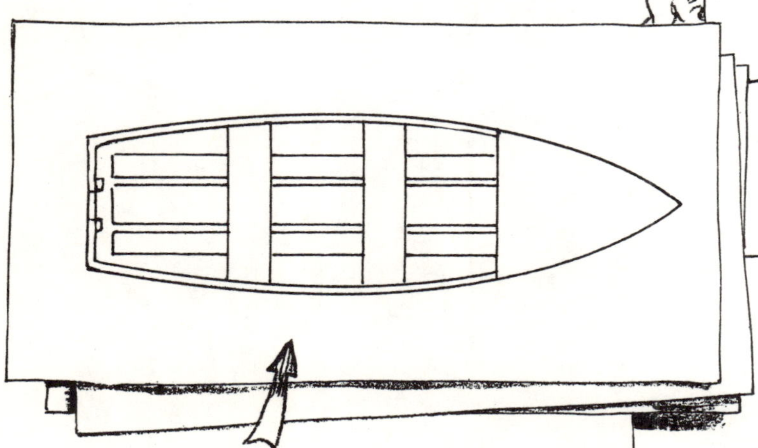

A PLAN OR A DIAGRAM IS FLAT.

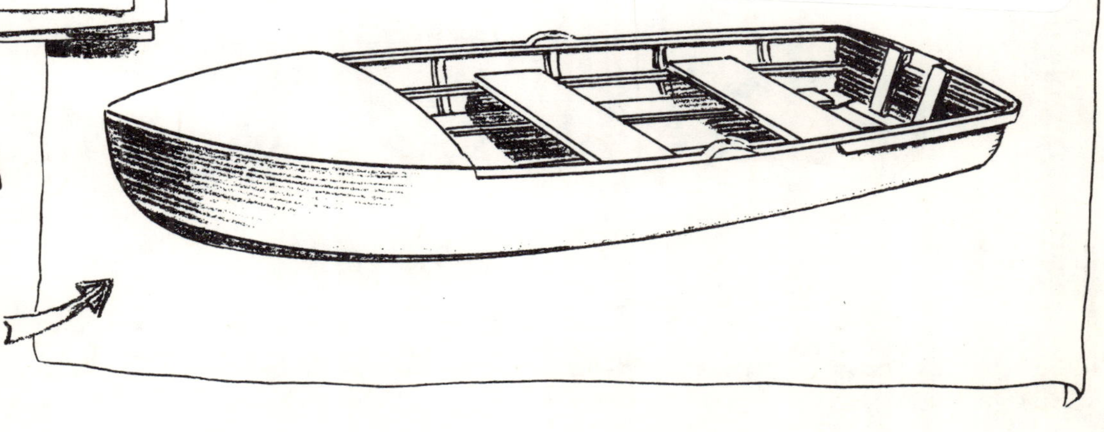

A PERSPECTIVE DRAWING APPEARS SOLID.

IT ISN'T HARD TO DRAW A BOX IN DIFFERENT POSITIONS—

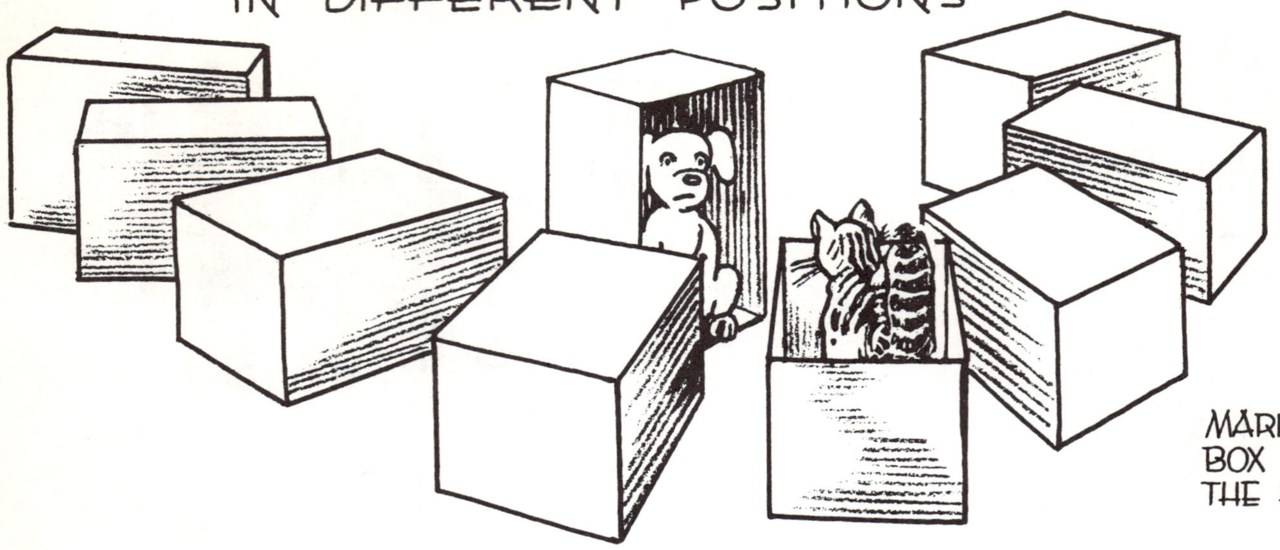

HAT IN A BOX

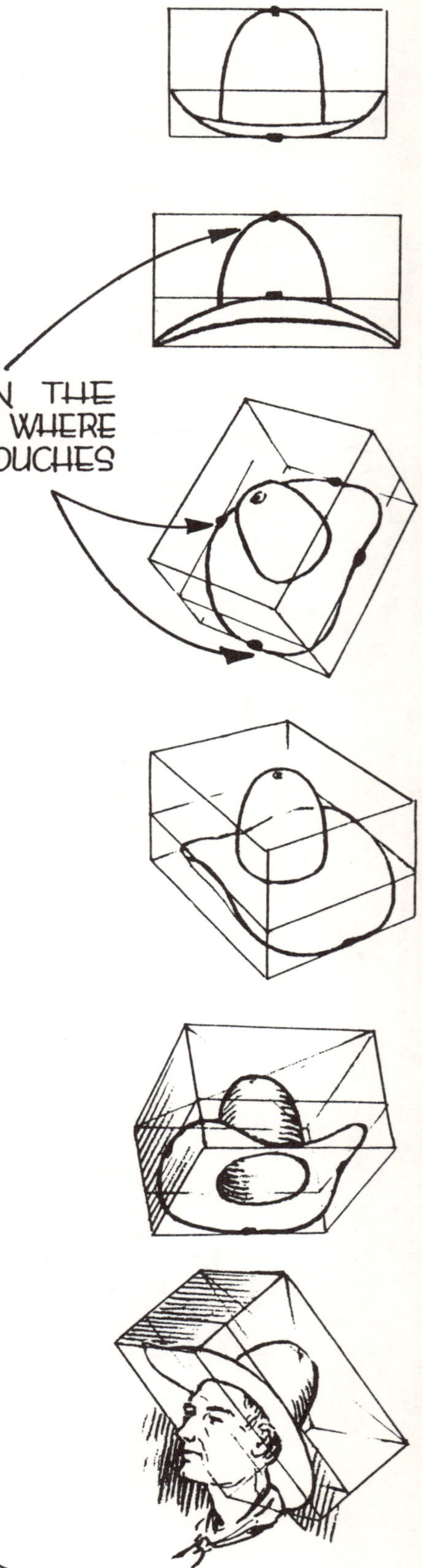

—OR THE SIDE VIEW OF A LAZY CAT

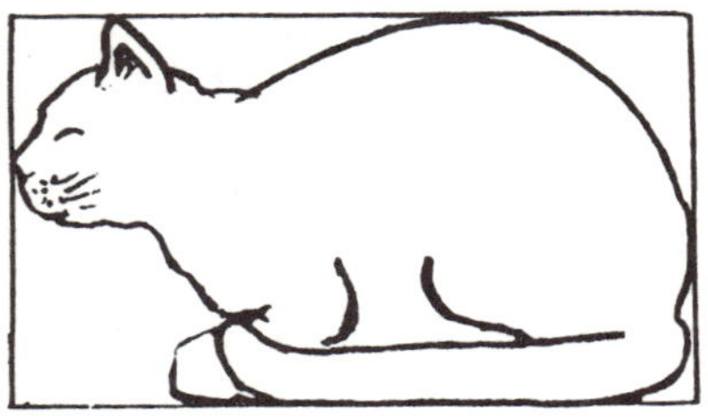

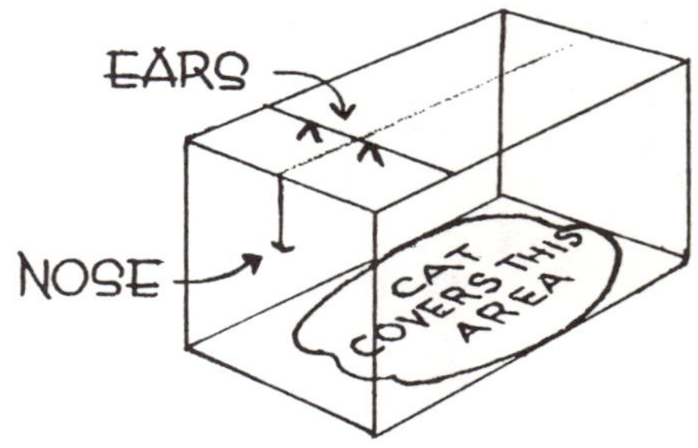

NOW HERE IS AN EASY WAY TO MAKE PERSPECTIVE DRAWINGS OF THE CAT —— JUST PUT THE CAT IN AN IMAGINARY BOX.

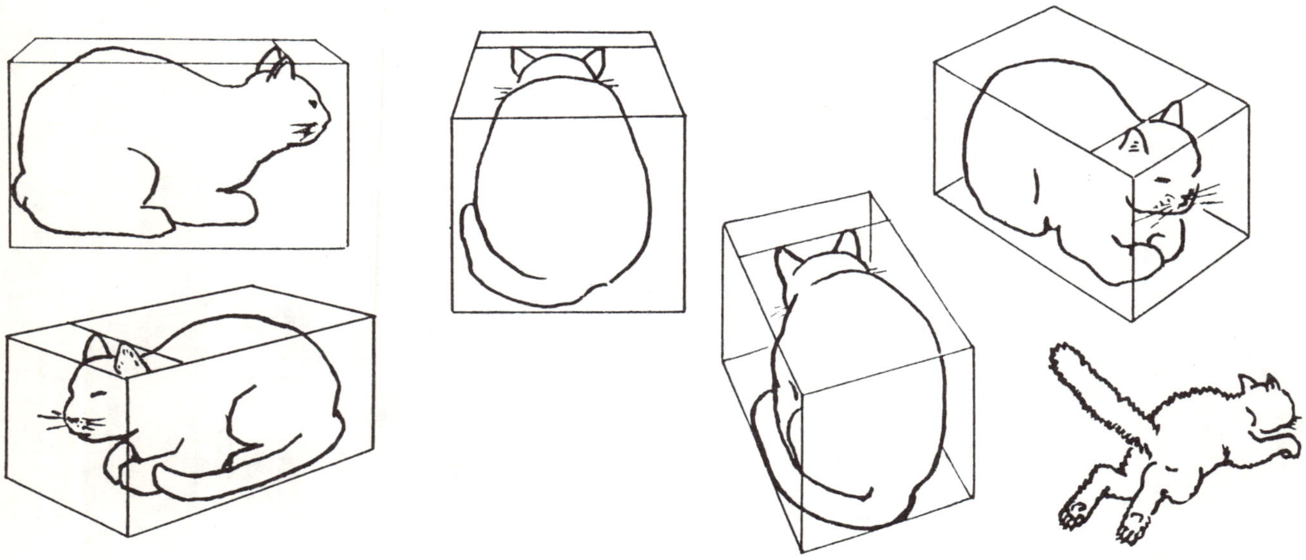

YOU WILL FIND THAT MANY THINGS CAN BE EASILY DRAWN IN PERSPECTIVE BY PLACING THEM IN BOXES.

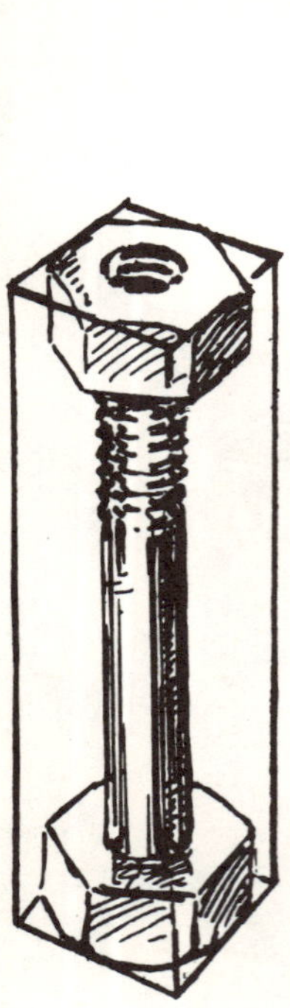

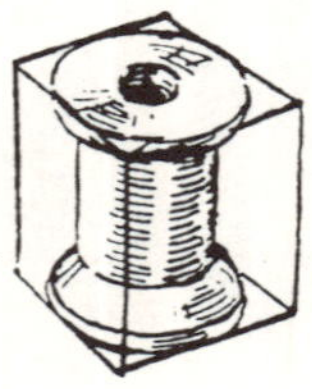

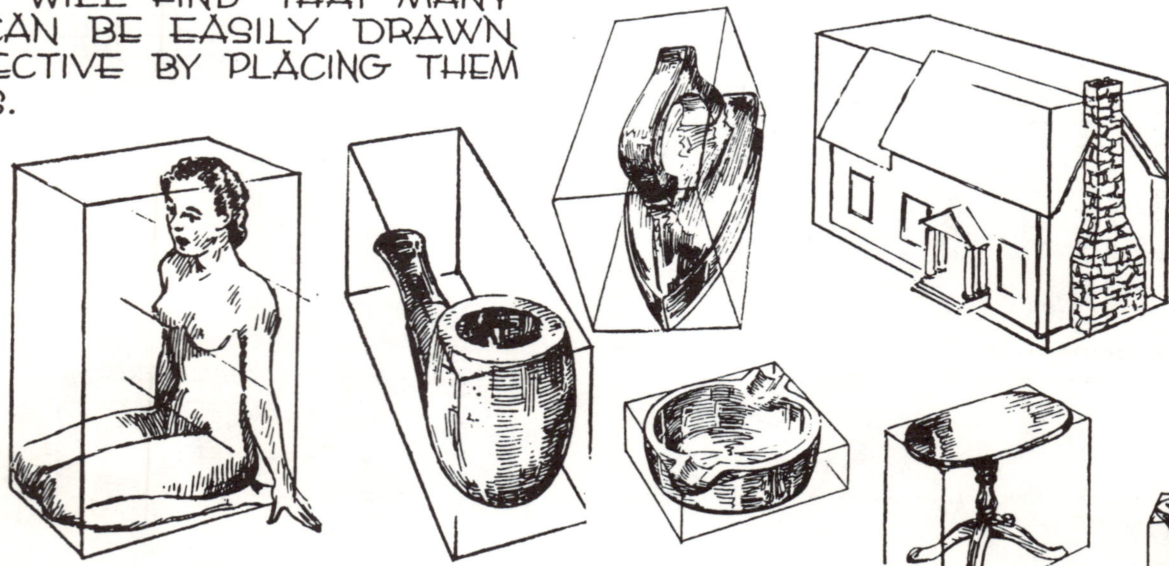

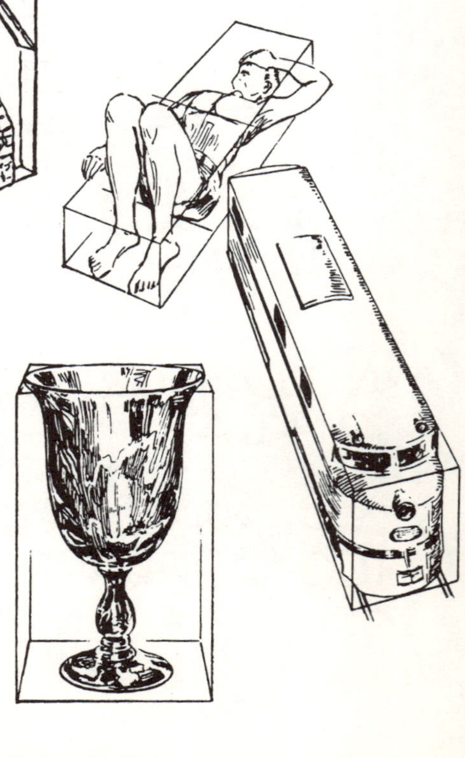

TRY IT!

IF THE PERSPECTIVE OF THE BOX IS CORRECT, THE THING INSIDE WILL BE BASED ON ACCURACY.

BEFORE DRAWING A BOX LET US INVESTIGATE THE EYE LEVEL

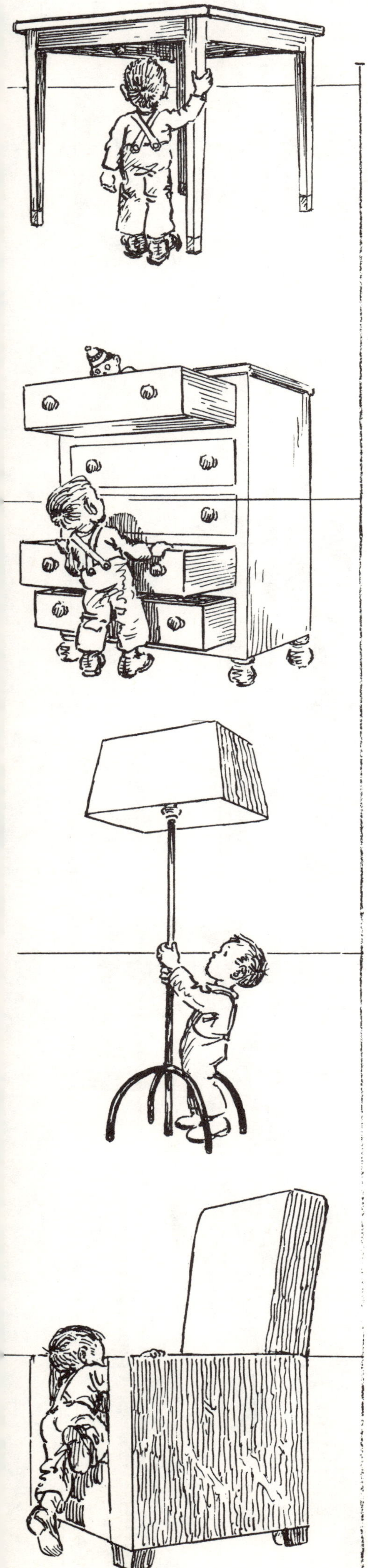

A CHILD'S EYE LEVEL

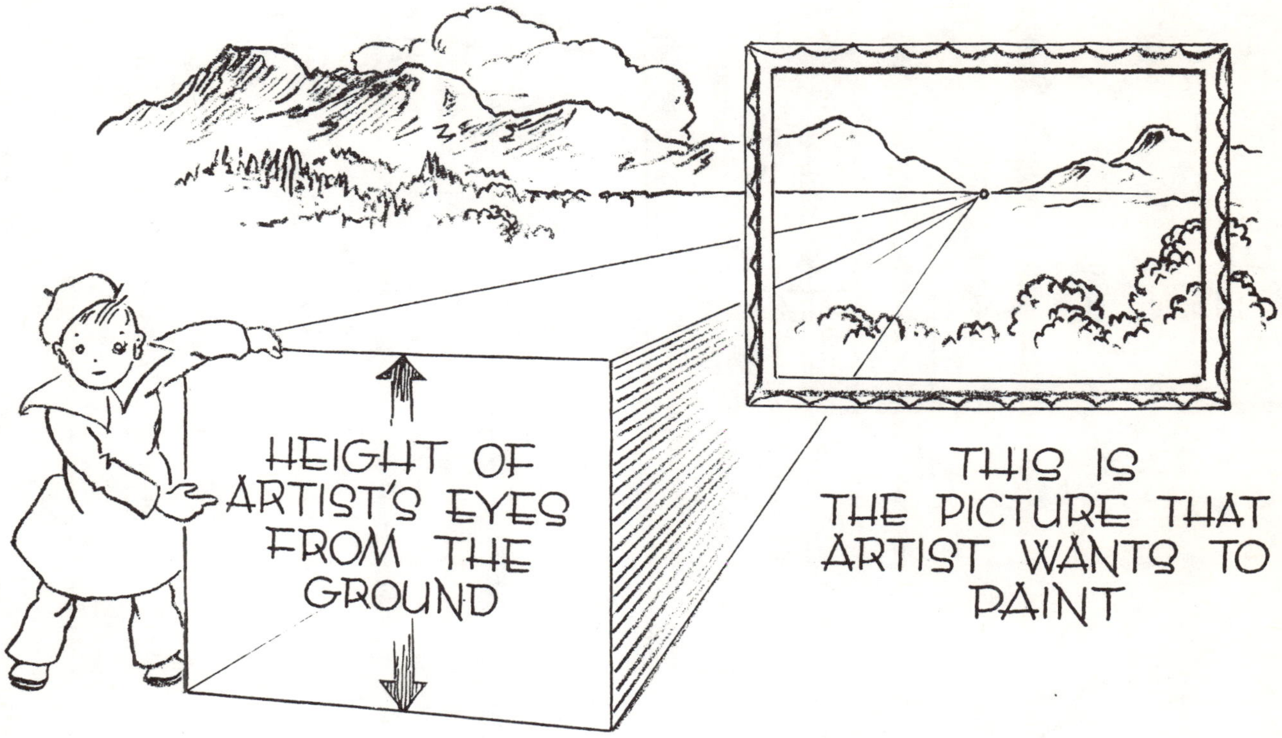

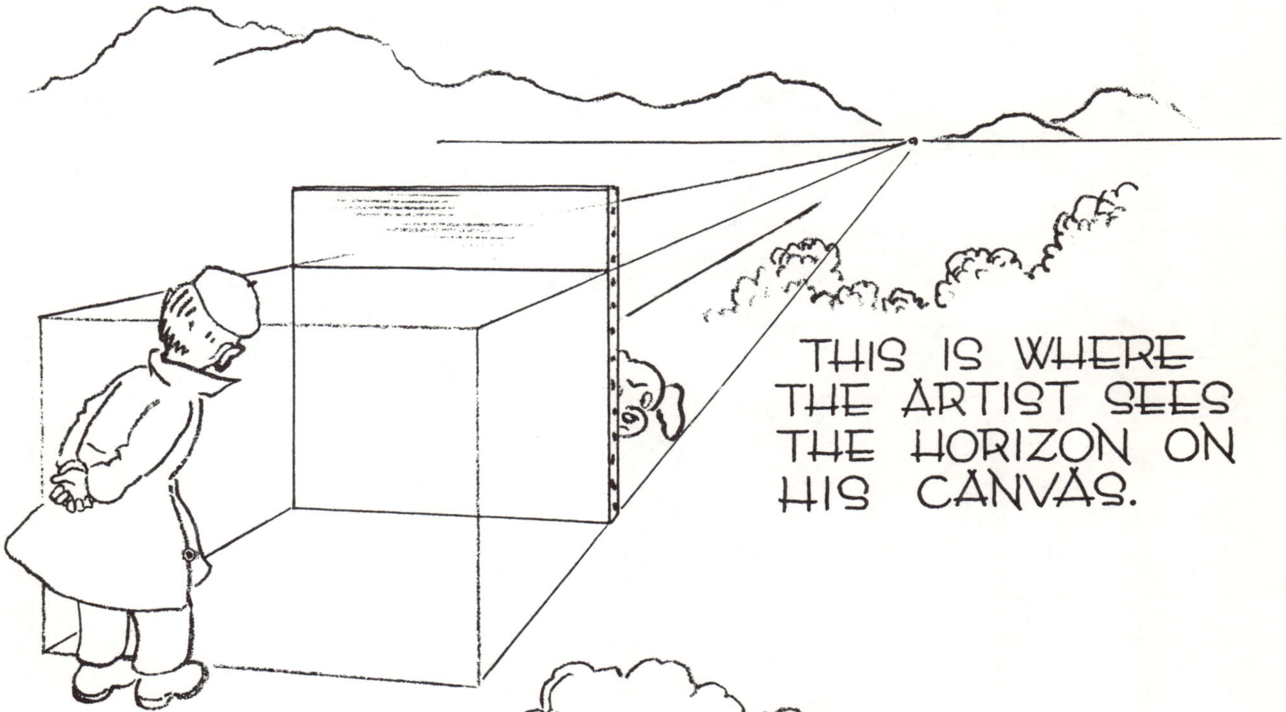

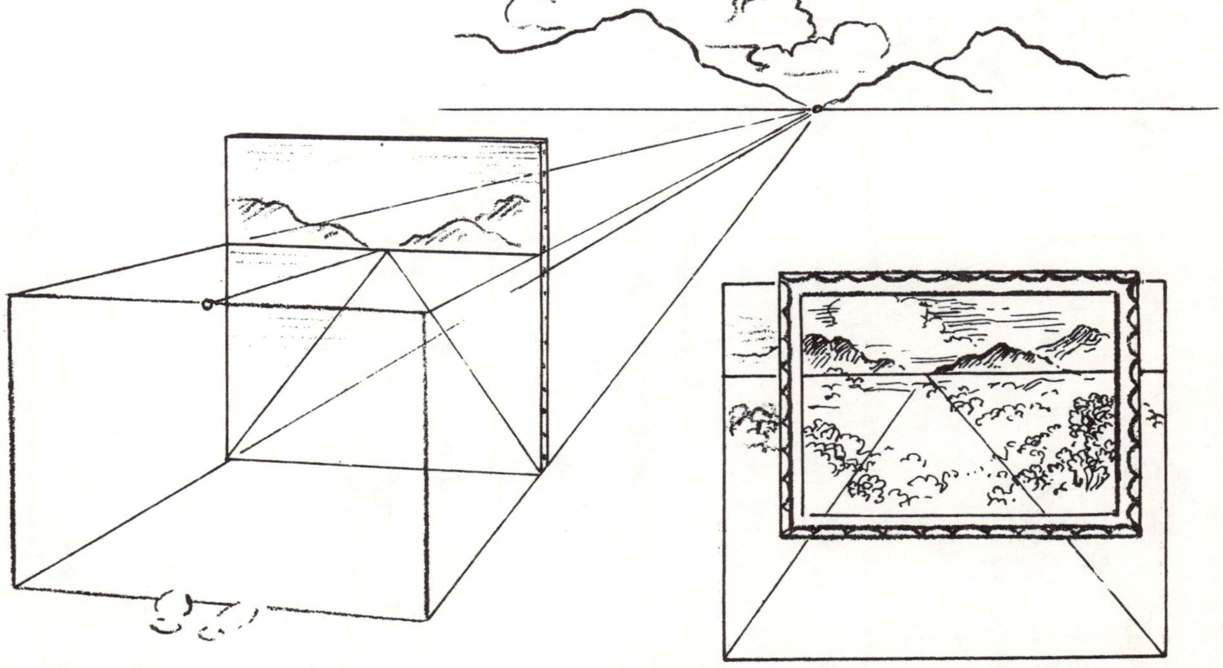

THE FINISHED PICTURE

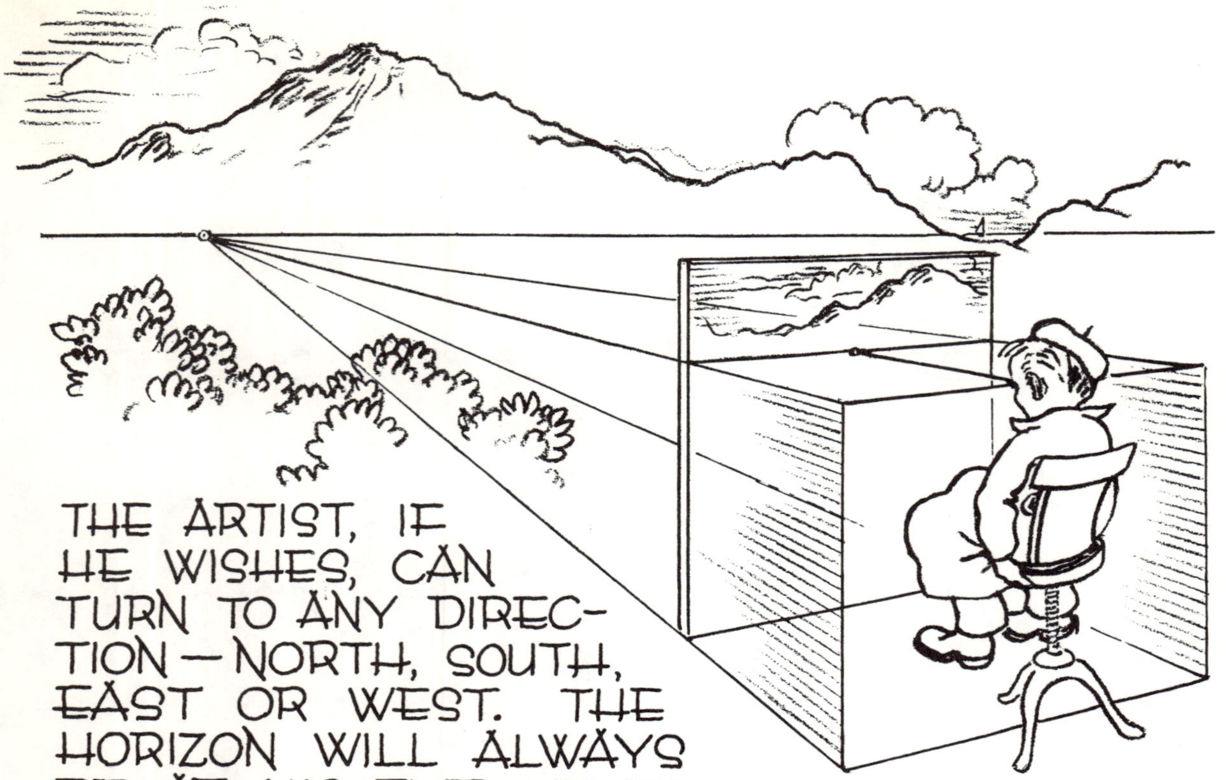

THE ARTIST, IF HE WISHES, CAN TURN TO ANY DIRECTION—NORTH, SOUTH, EAST OR WEST. THE HORIZON WILL ALWAYS BE AT HIS EYE LEVEL.

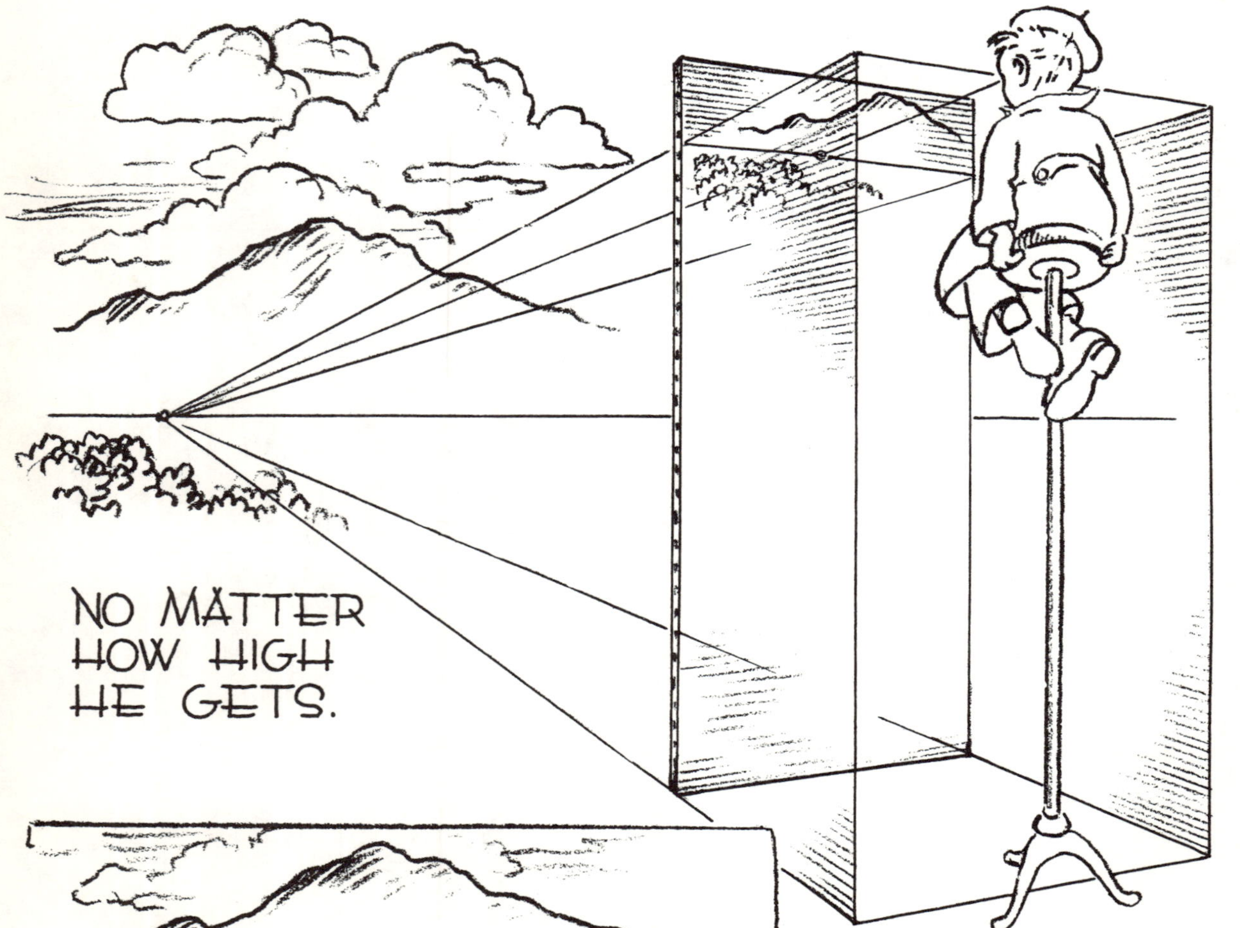

NO MATTER HOW HIGH HE GETS.

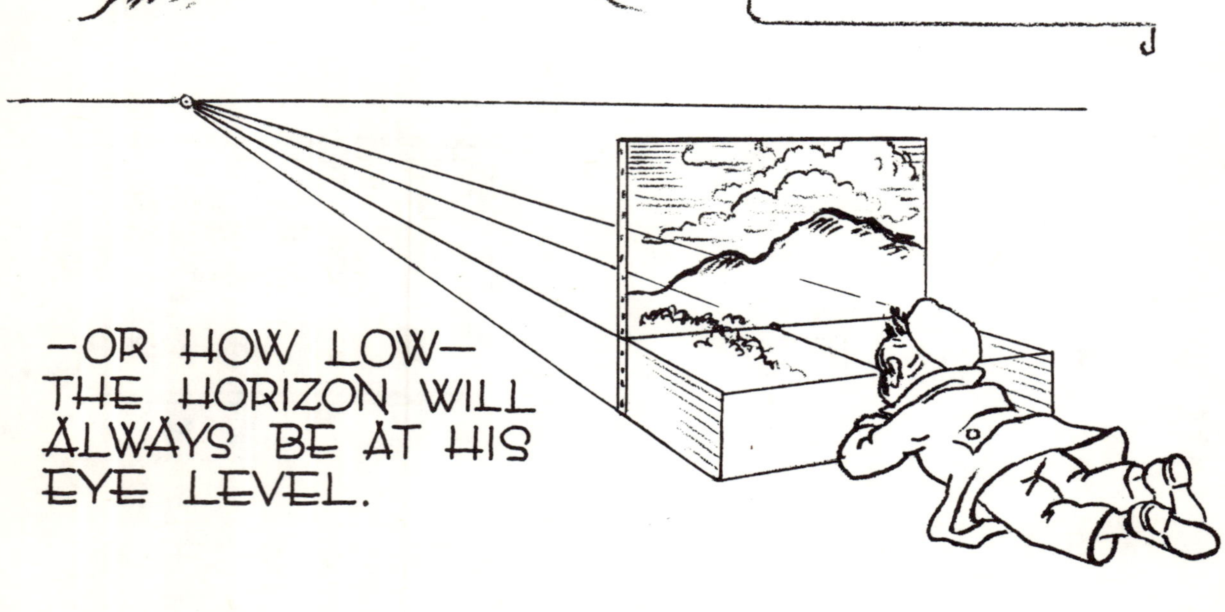

—OR HOW LOW— THE HORIZON WILL ALWAYS BE AT HIS EYE LEVEL.

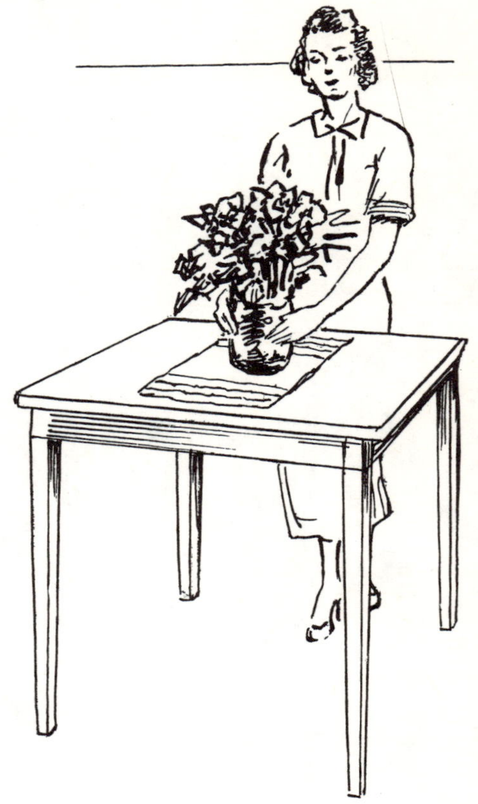

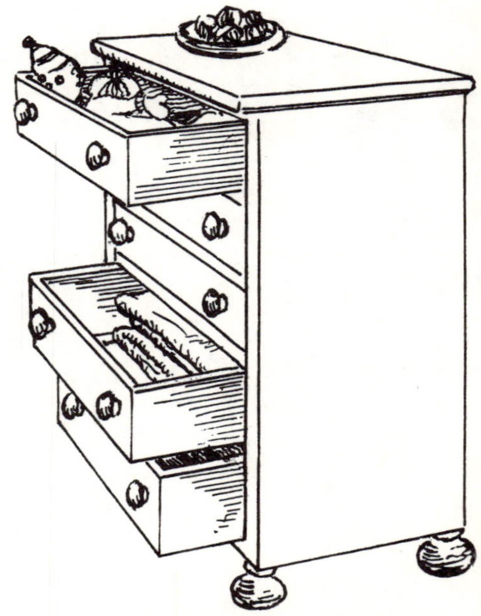

A GROWN UP'S EYE LEVEL

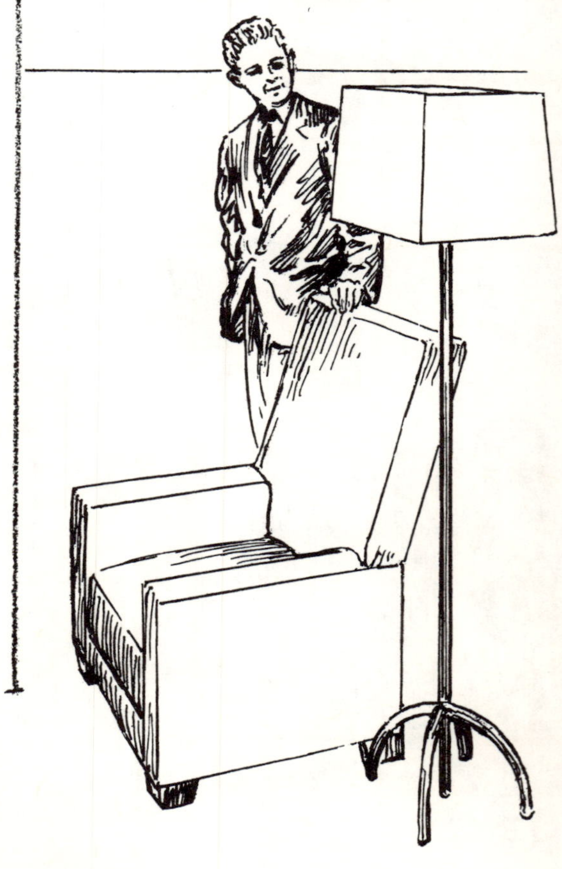

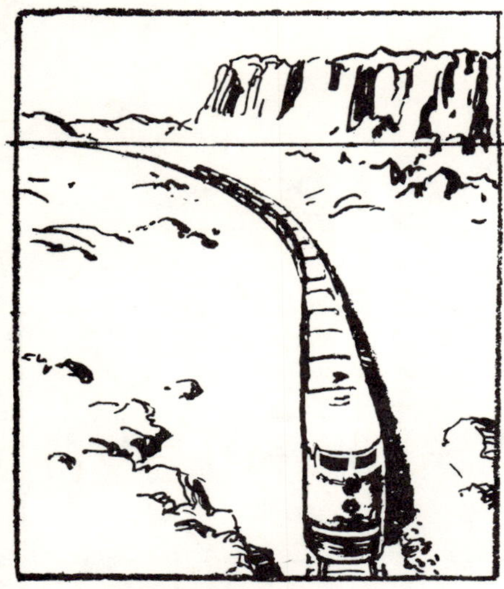

BIRDSEYE

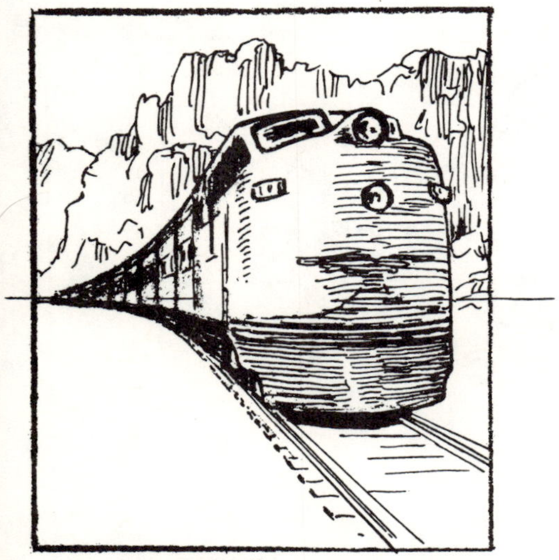

NORMAL VIEW

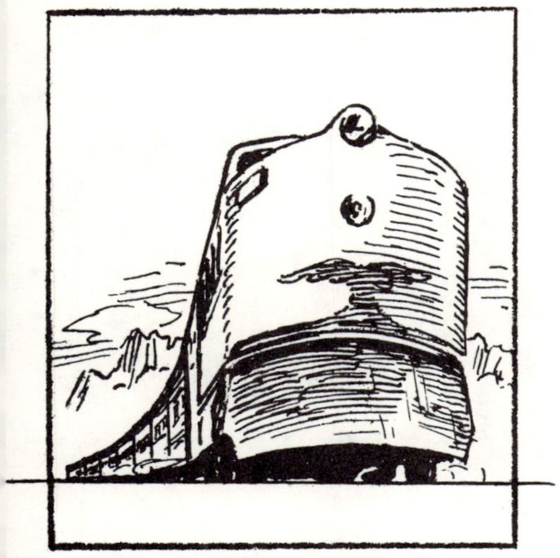

WORMSEYE

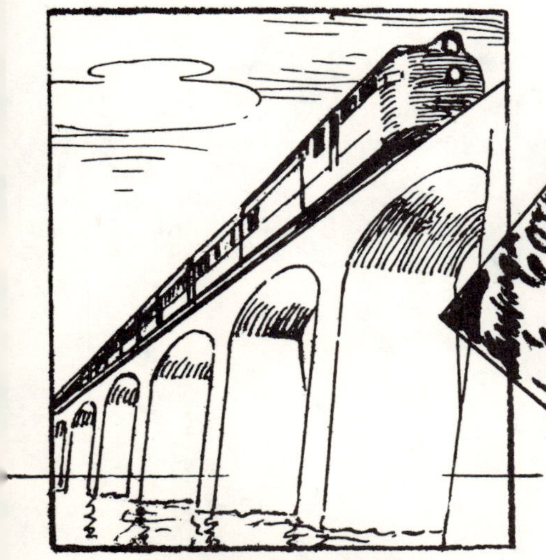

OVERHEAD

FROM A BALLOON

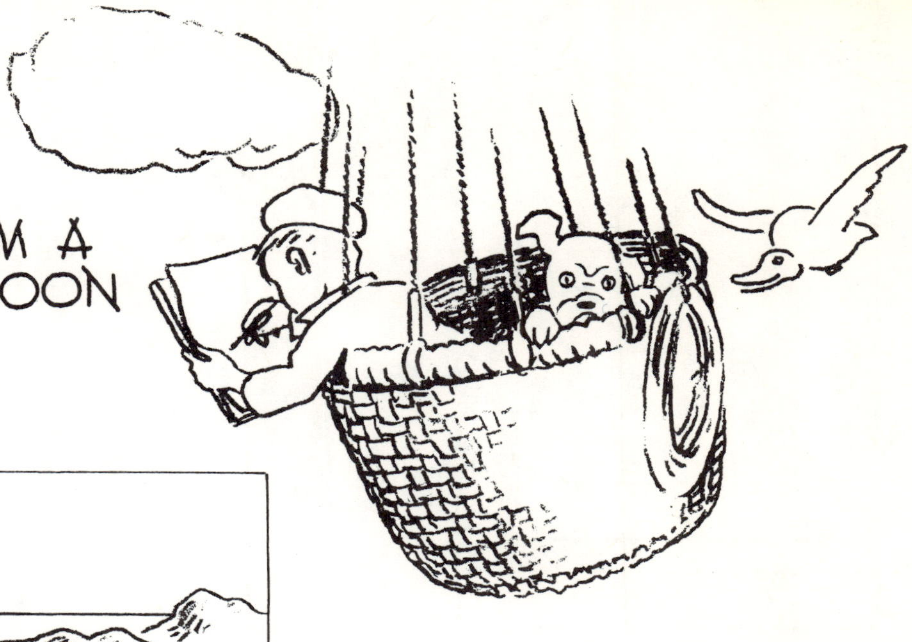

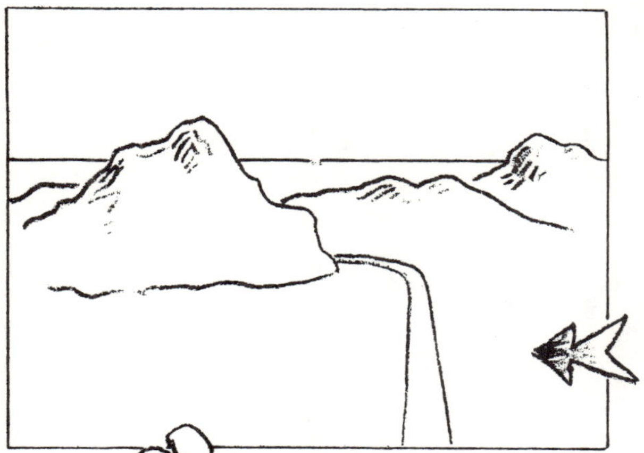

HIS PICTURE WILL LOOK LIKE THIS

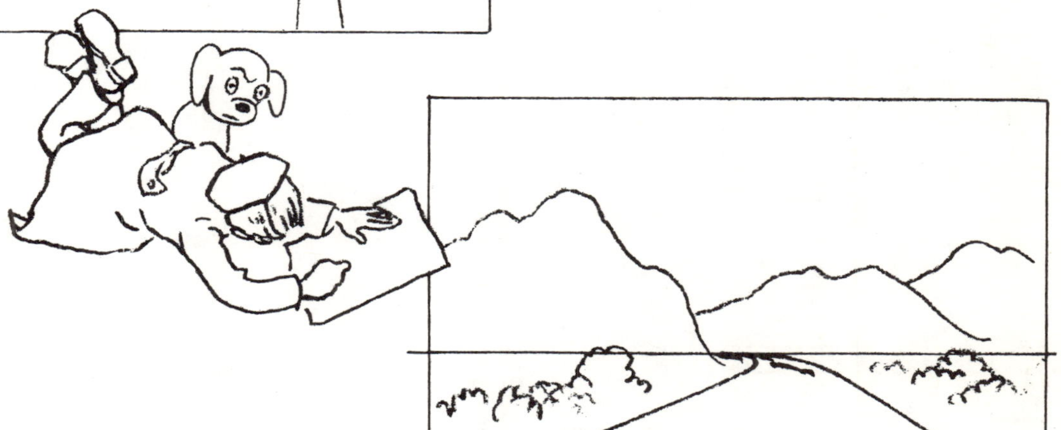

AND FROM THE GROUND—
HIS PICTURE WILL LOOK THIS WAY

HE FINDS THAT IN BOTH INSTANCES THE HORIZON IS LEVEL WITH HIS EYES. HE DRAWS IT AS A STRAIGHT LINE ACROSS HIS PICTURE AND—

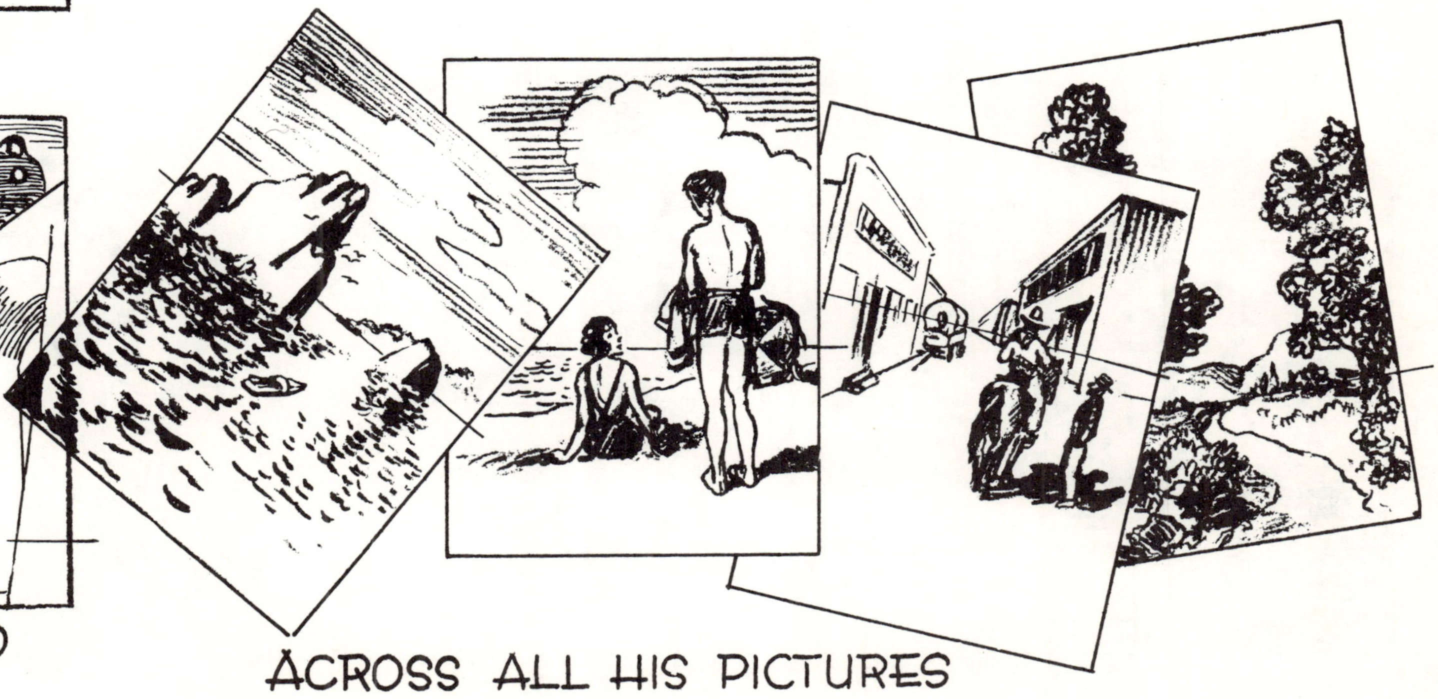

ACROSS ALL HIS PICTURES

THE VANISHING POINT

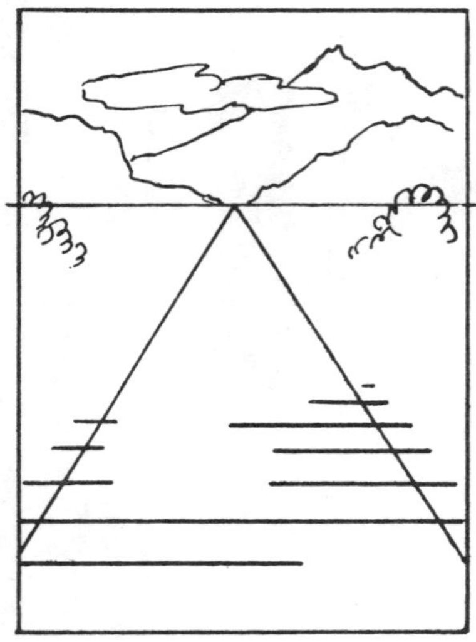

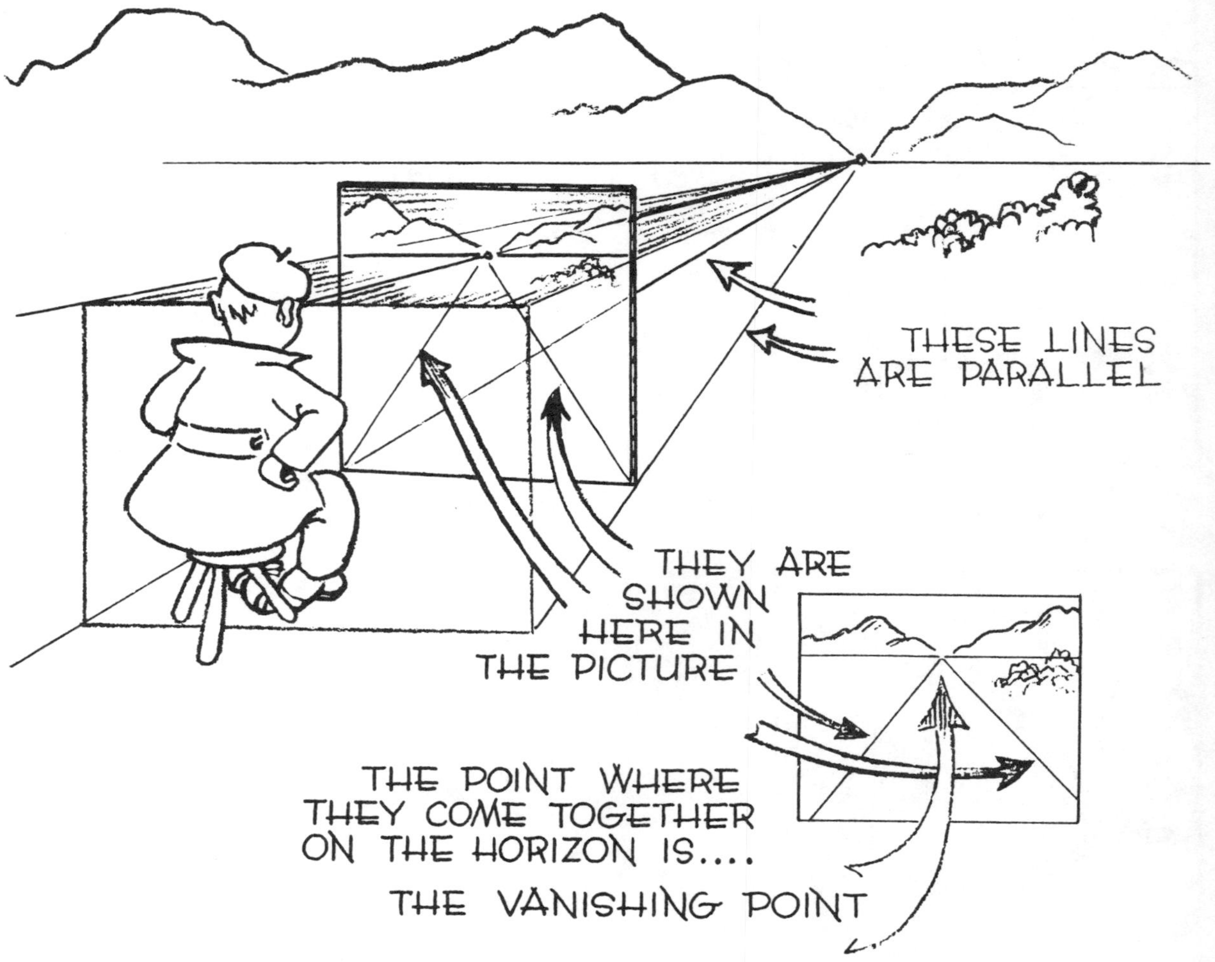

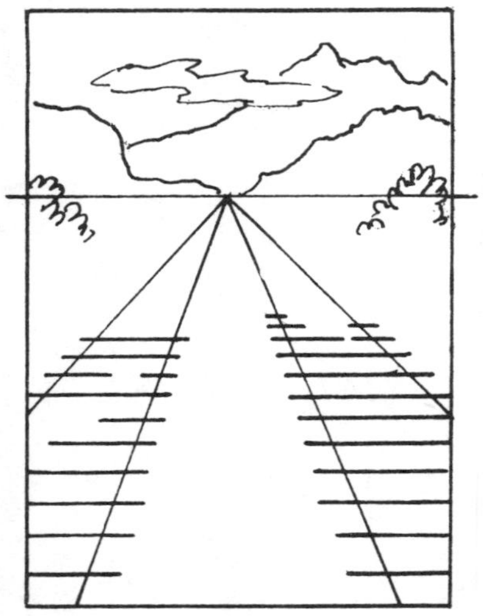

IF OTHER PARALLEL LINES ARE DRAWN THEY WILL COME TOGETHER ON THE PICTURE AT THE SAME VANISHING POINT

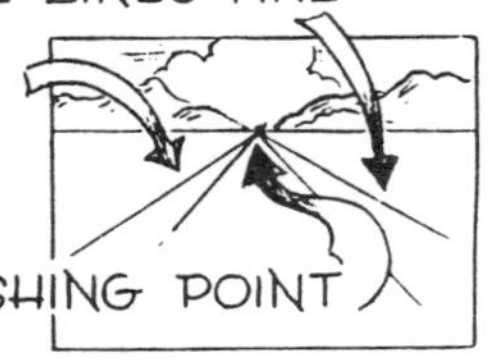

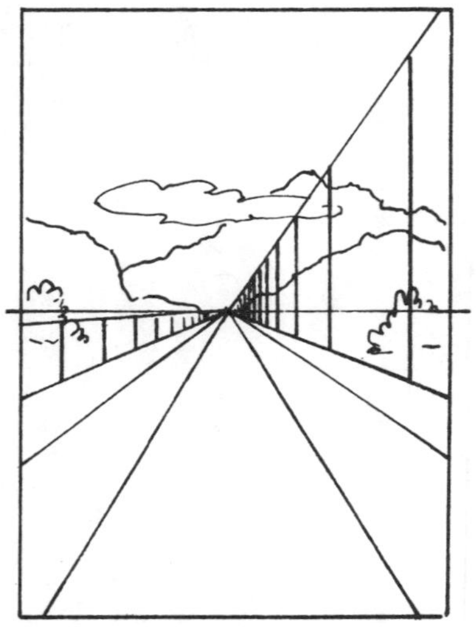

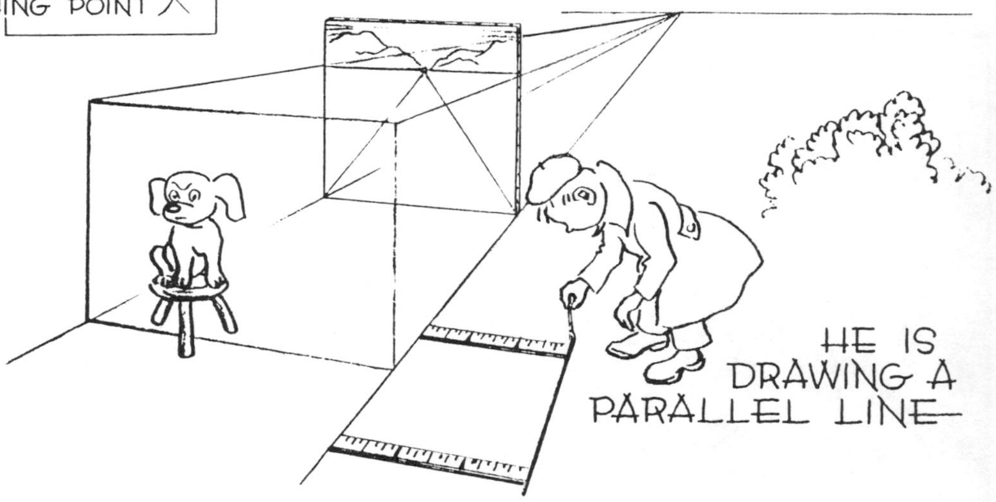

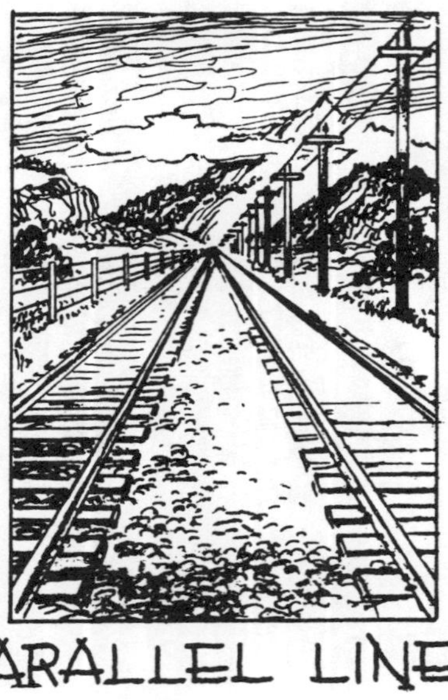

PARALLEL LINES

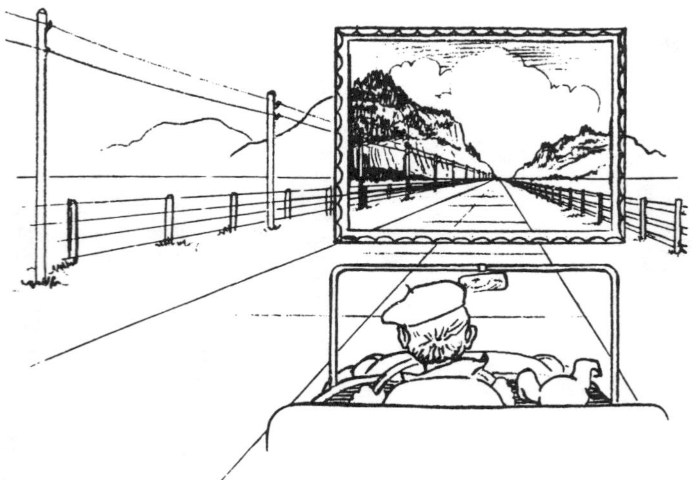

WHEN YOU ARE DRIVING ON THE HIGHWAY, NOTICE THE PICTURE STRAIGHT AHEAD.
THE HIGHWAY, THE FENCES, THE TELEPHONE LINES —ALL GO TO ONE VANISHING POINT.

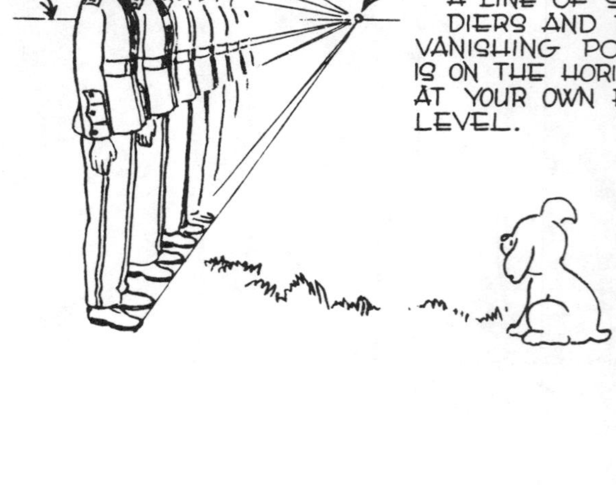

THE SOLDIERS DO TOO. IF YOU CAN DRAW ONE SOLDIER YOU CAN DRAW A LINE OF SOLDIERS AND THE VANISHING POINT IS ON THE HORIZON AT YOUR OWN EYE LEVEL.

STUDY THIS DIAGRAM SHOWING HOW TO USE THE VANISHING POINTS AND EYE LEVEL TO LAYOUT THE INTERIOR OF A ROOM.

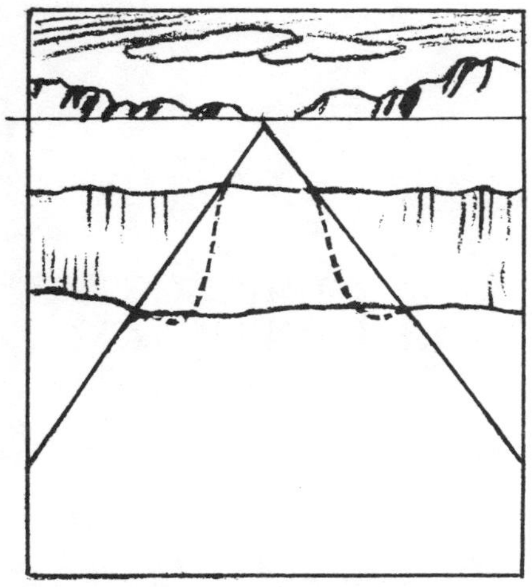

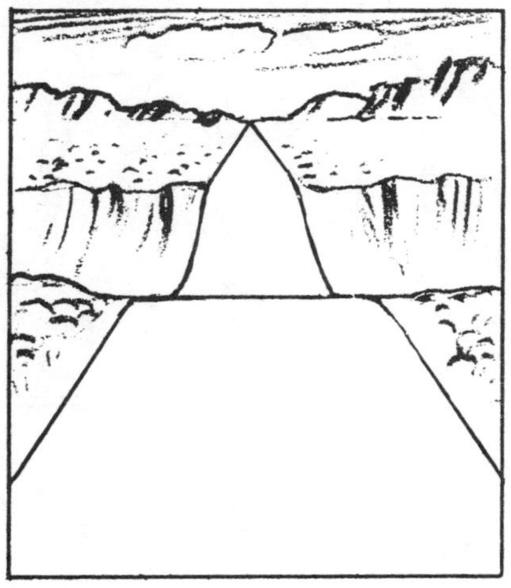

THERE IS A DIP IN THE HIGHWAY

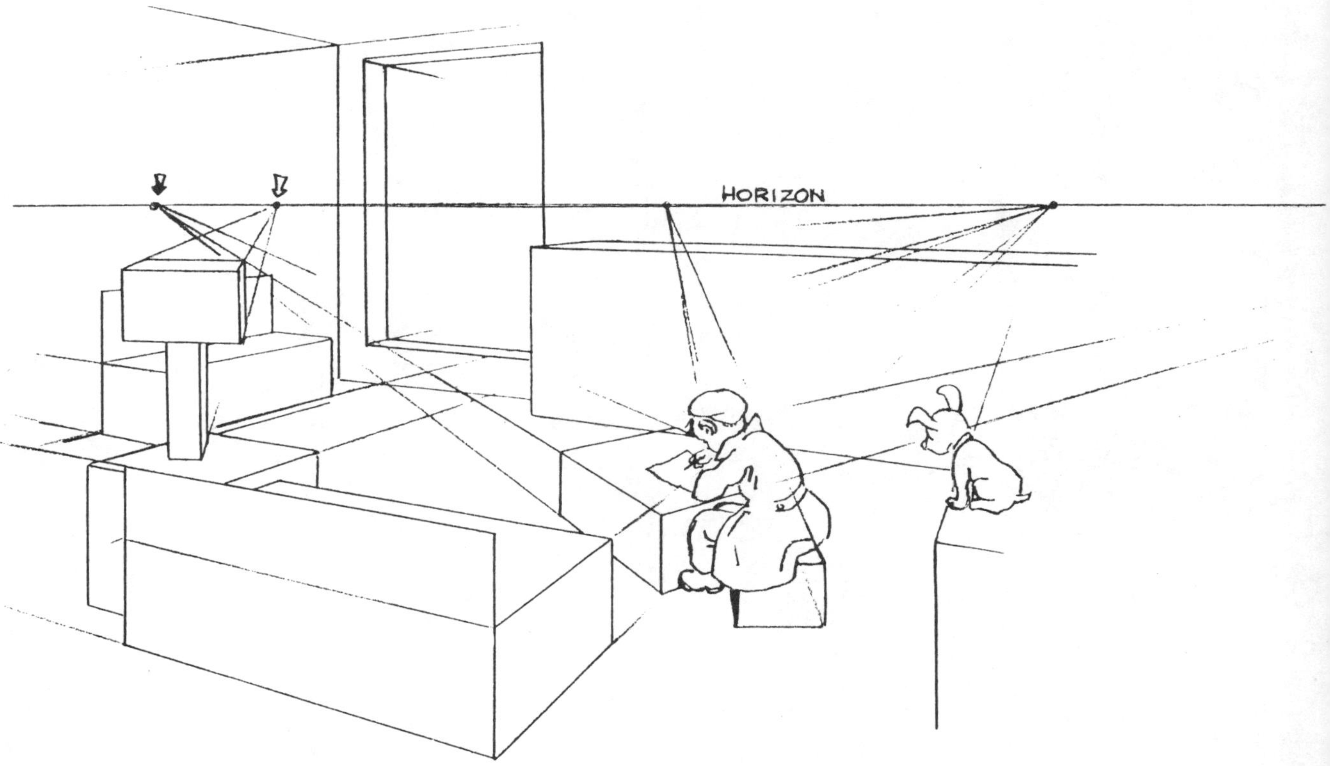

NOW, LET'S DRAW A ROOM USING THE VANISHING POINTS SHOWN HERE.

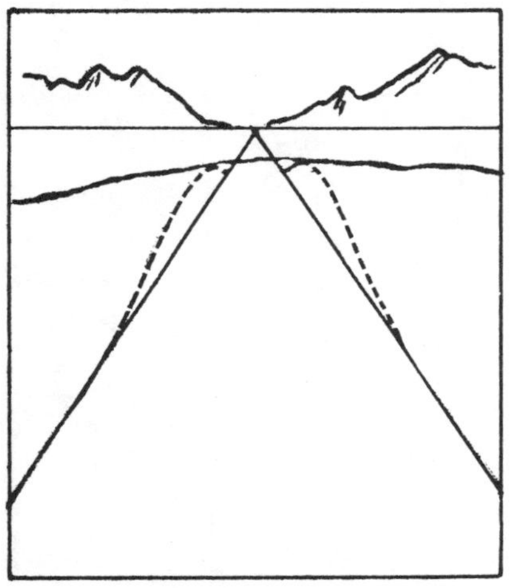

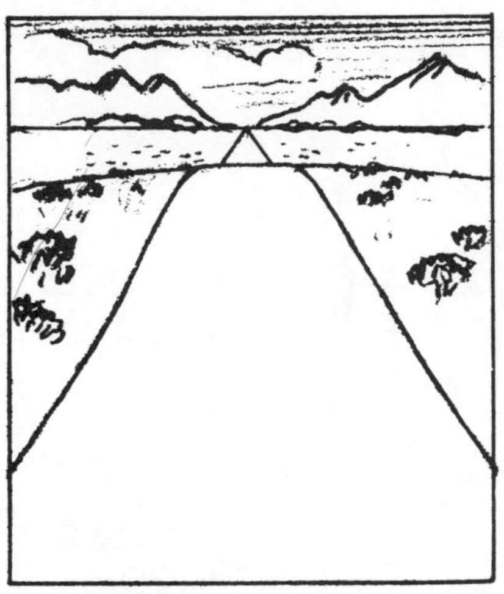

A RISE AHEAD

TEXTURING TECHNIQUES MAKE THE ROOM APPEAR MORE SOLID.

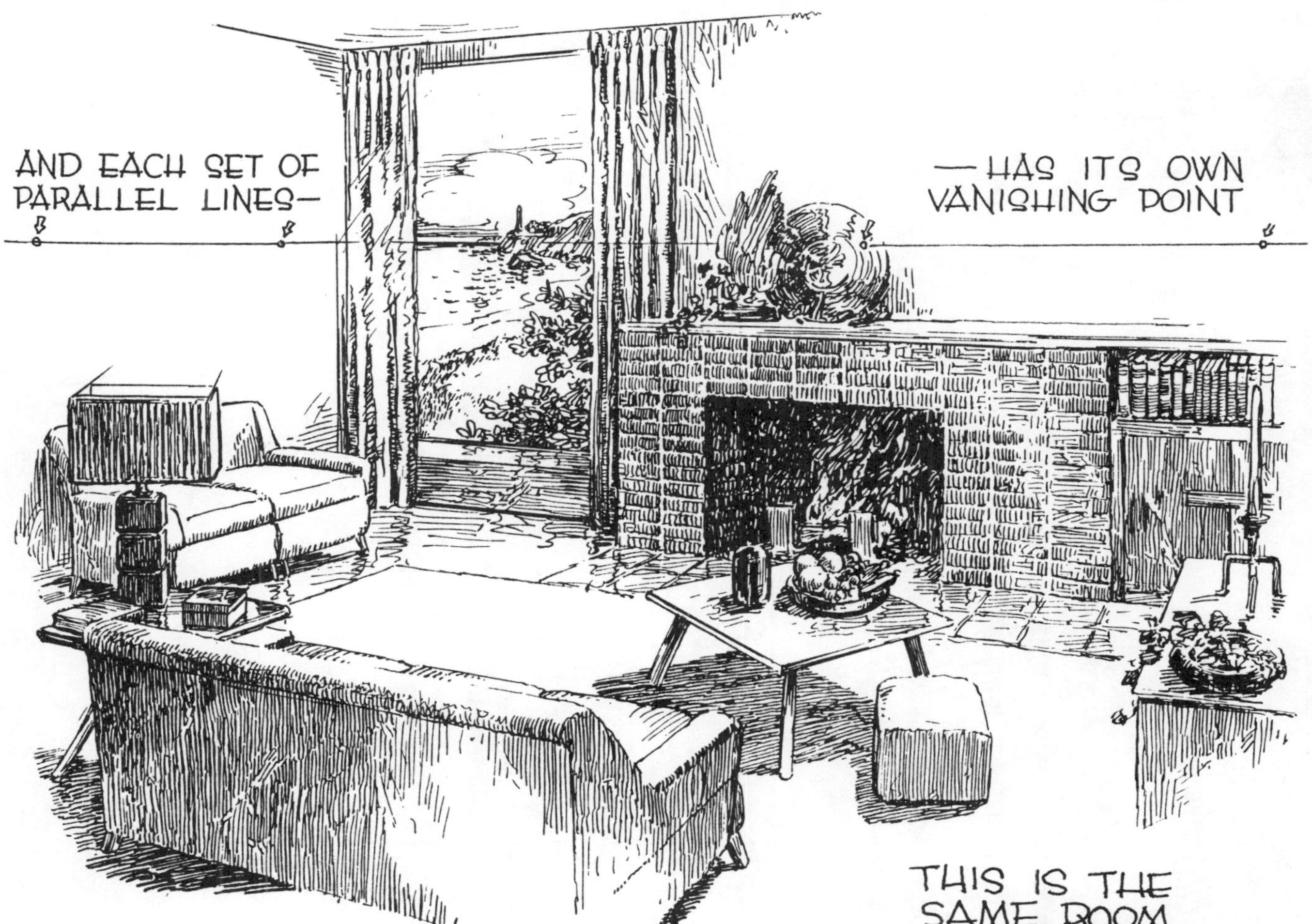

THIS IS THE SAME ROOM SHOWN ABOVE.

WE HAVE FOUND BOXES USEFUL AIDS IN DRAWING

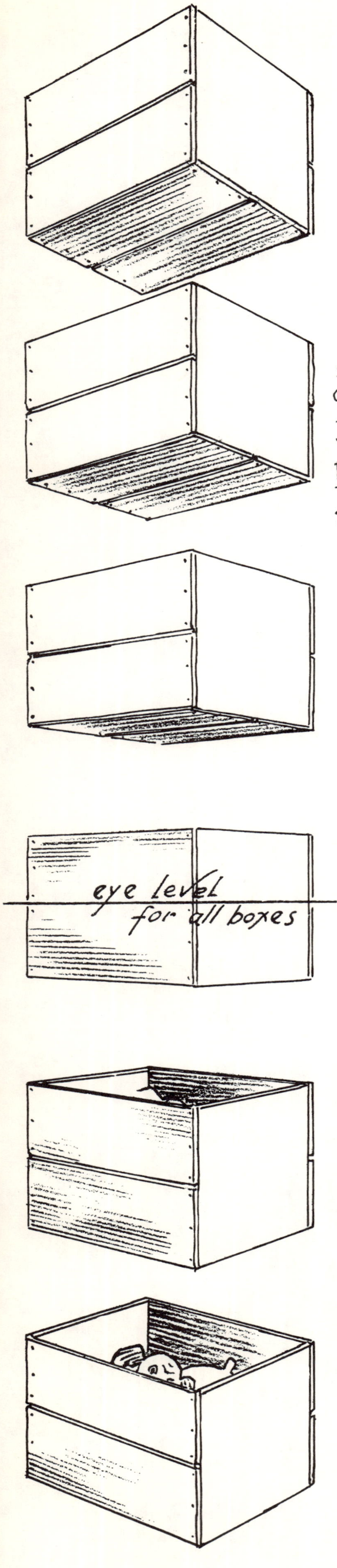

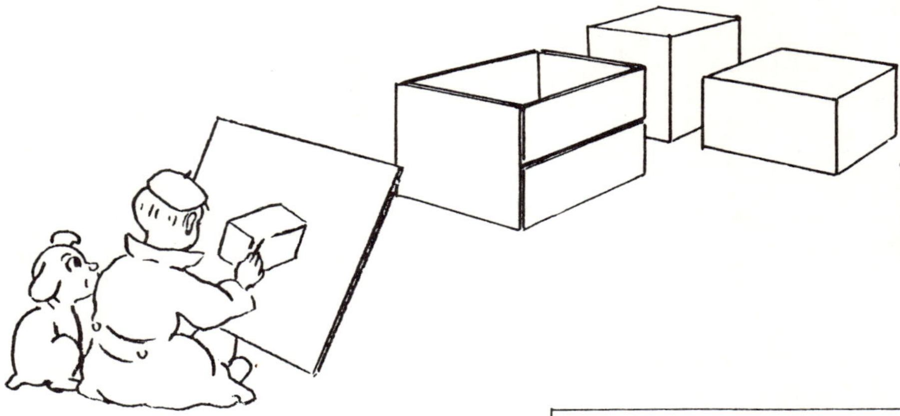

SO NOW LET US LEARN HOW TO DRAW THEM

SKETCH THE BOX AS CAREFULLY AS YOU CAN —JUST AS YOU SEE IT. YOU KNOW THAT ALL PARALLEL EDGES EXTEND TO A VANISHING POINT— SO TAKE THE SKETCH

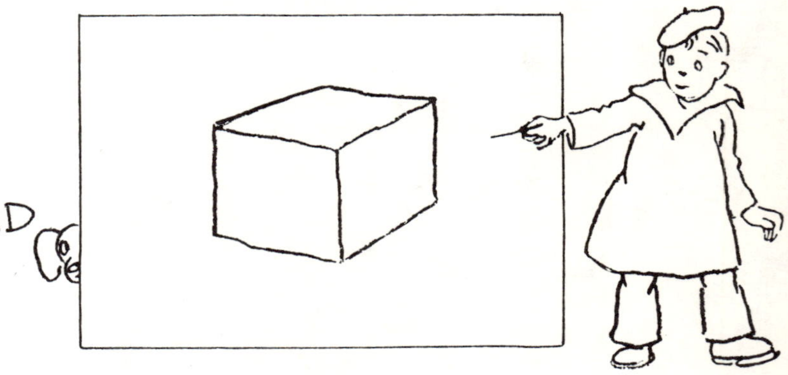

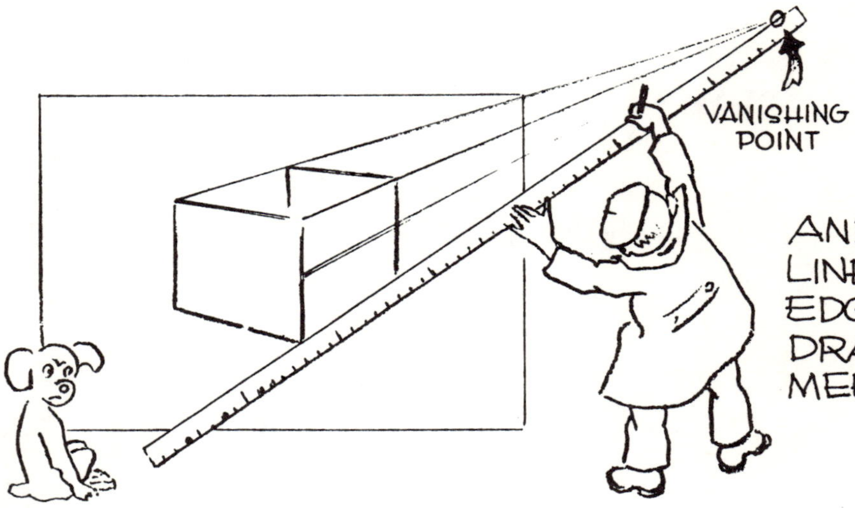

AND DRAW STRAIGHT LINES FROM THESE EDGES. CORRECT THE DRAWING SO THE LINES MEET AT ONE POINT.

AFTER ONE OF THE VANISHING POINTS HAS BEEN FOUND, THE REST IS EASY.

THE HORIZON MUST BE LEVEL AND IT MUST PASS THROUGH THAT POINT.
SO DRAW THE HORIZON LINE THROUGH THE POINT AND ACROSS THE PAPER.

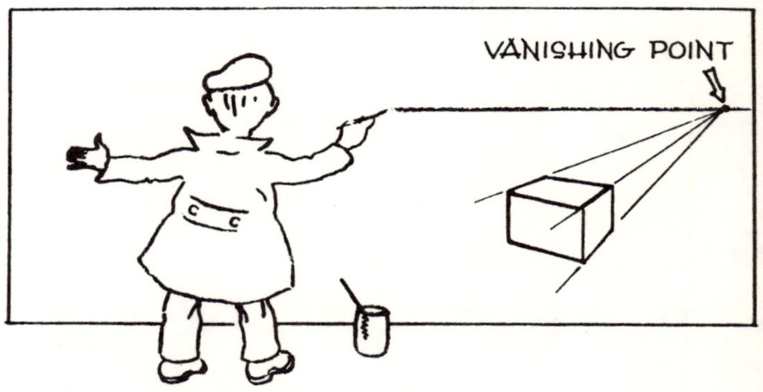

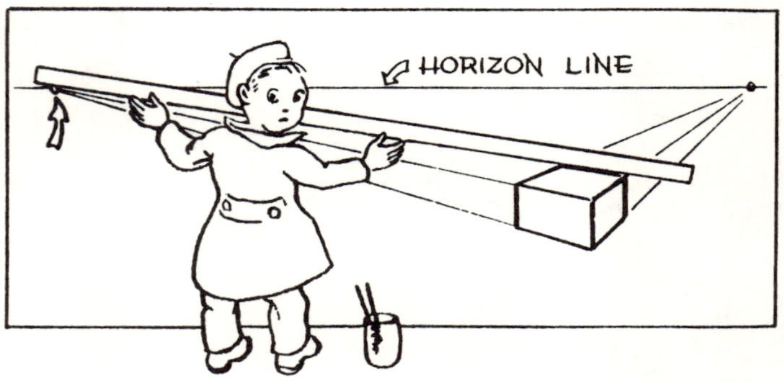

THE OTHER PARALLEL LINES OF THE BOX CAN NOW BE EXTENDED. THEY SHOULD MEET ON THIS LINE. THIS GIVES US THE OTHER VANISHING POINT FOR THE BOX.

A SNAPSHOT OR A PICTURE FROM A MAGAZINE

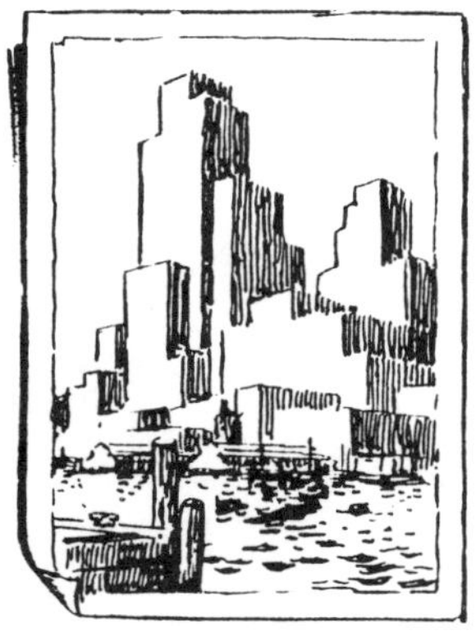

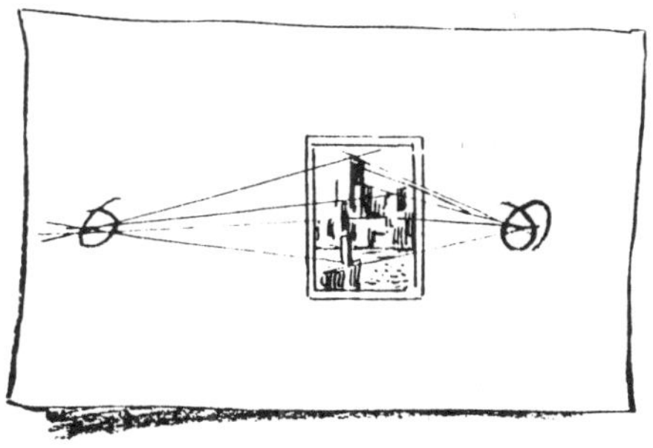

PASTE IT ON A LARGE SHEET OF PAPER— EXTEND THE PERSPECTIVE LINES THE TWO POINTS AND THE HORIZON CAN BE LOCATED.

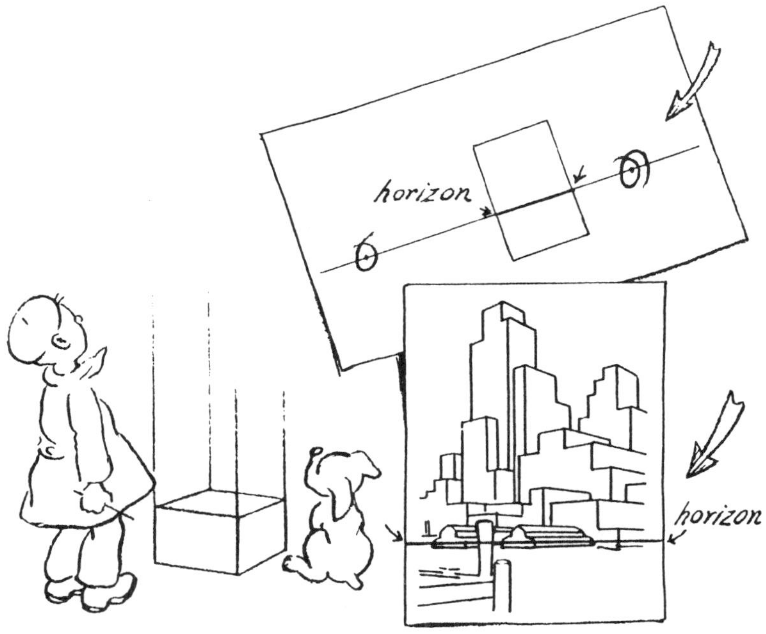

THE PERPENDICULAR LINES DO NOT COME TOGETHER. THEY HAVE NO VANISHING POINT.

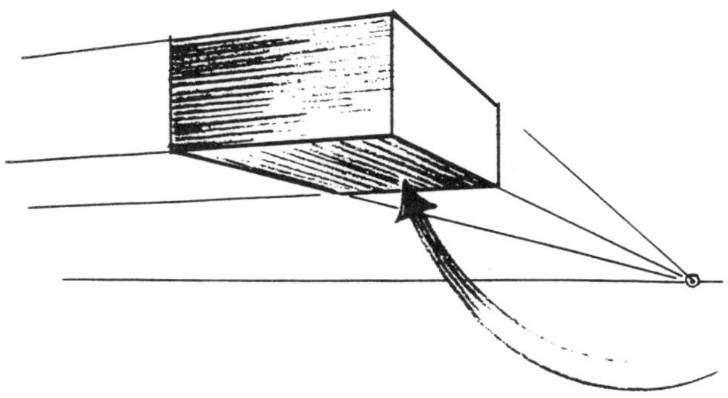

IF THE BOX IS ABOVE THE EYE LEVEL YOU WILL SEE IT'S UNDER-SIDE

TABLES ARE SEEN WITH THE EYE-LEVEL ABOVE

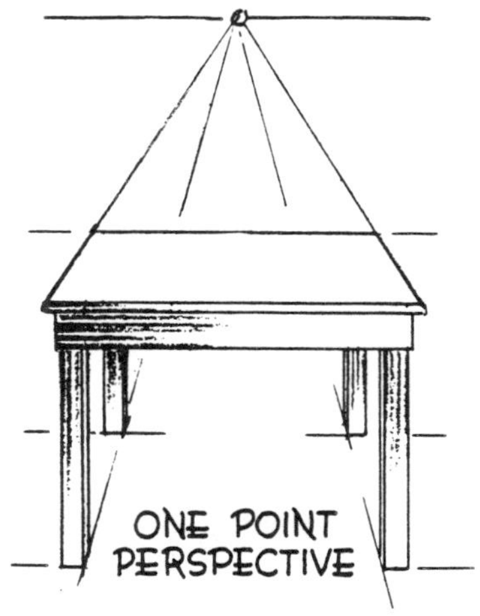

ONE POINT PERSPECTIVE

IF THE BOX IS BELOW THE EYE LEVEL (OR HORIZON LINE) YOU WILL SEE IT'S TOP

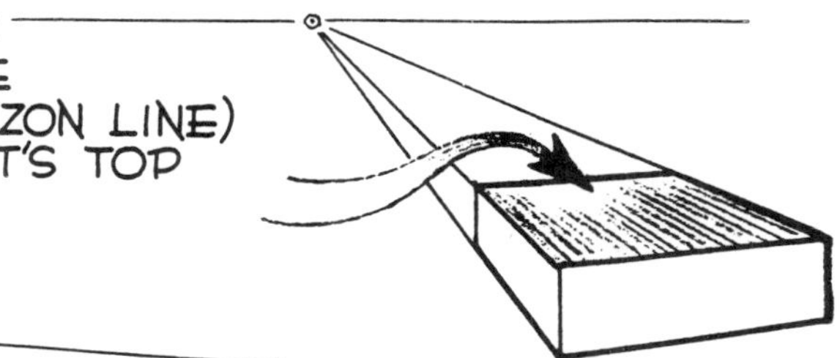

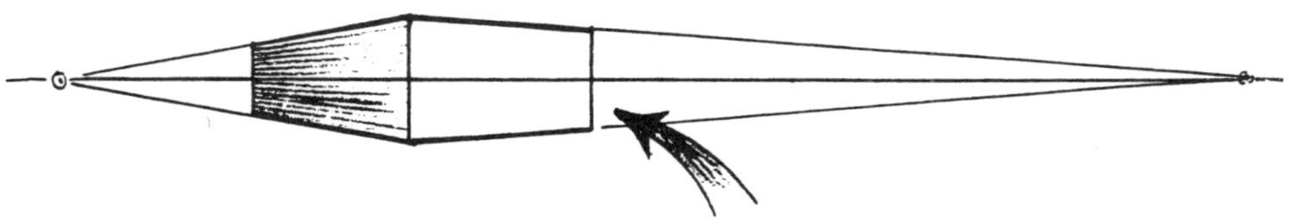

YOU SEE NEITHER TOP NOR BOTTOM IF THE BOX IS AT EYE LEVEL

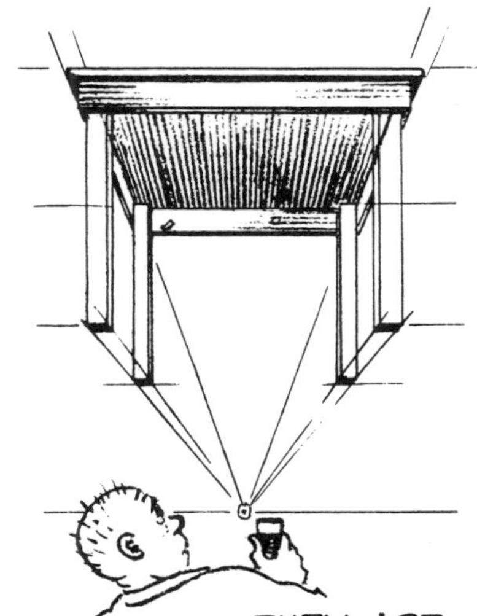

THEY ARE SELDOM SEEN WITH THE EYE-LEVEL BELOW

SMALL THINGS ARE USUALLY SHOWN BELOW YOUR EYE LEVEL

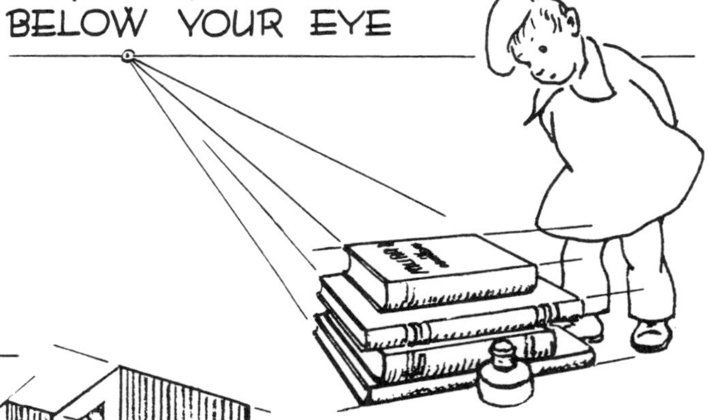

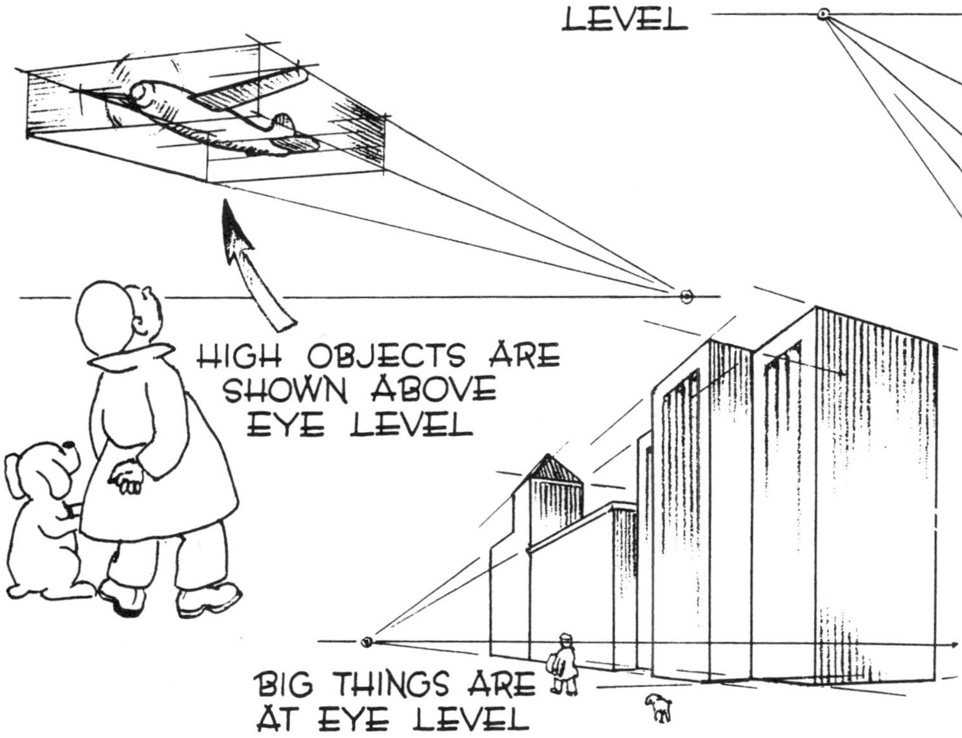

HIGH OBJECTS ARE SHOWN ABOVE EYE LEVEL

BIG THINGS ARE AT EYE LEVEL

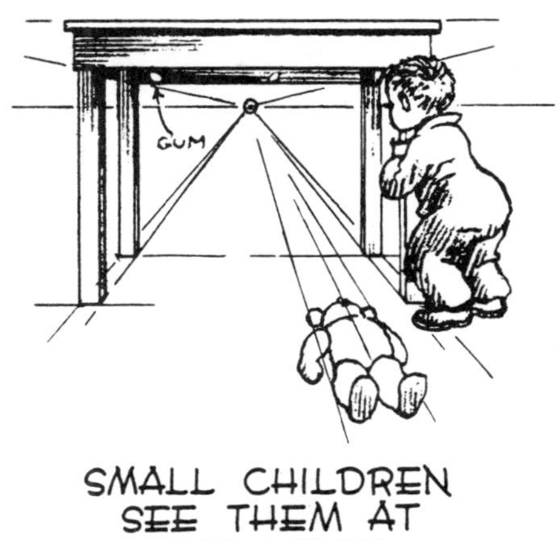

SMALL CHILDREN SEE THEM AT EYE-LEVEL

HIGH THINGS AS SEEN ABOVE THE EYE LEVEL

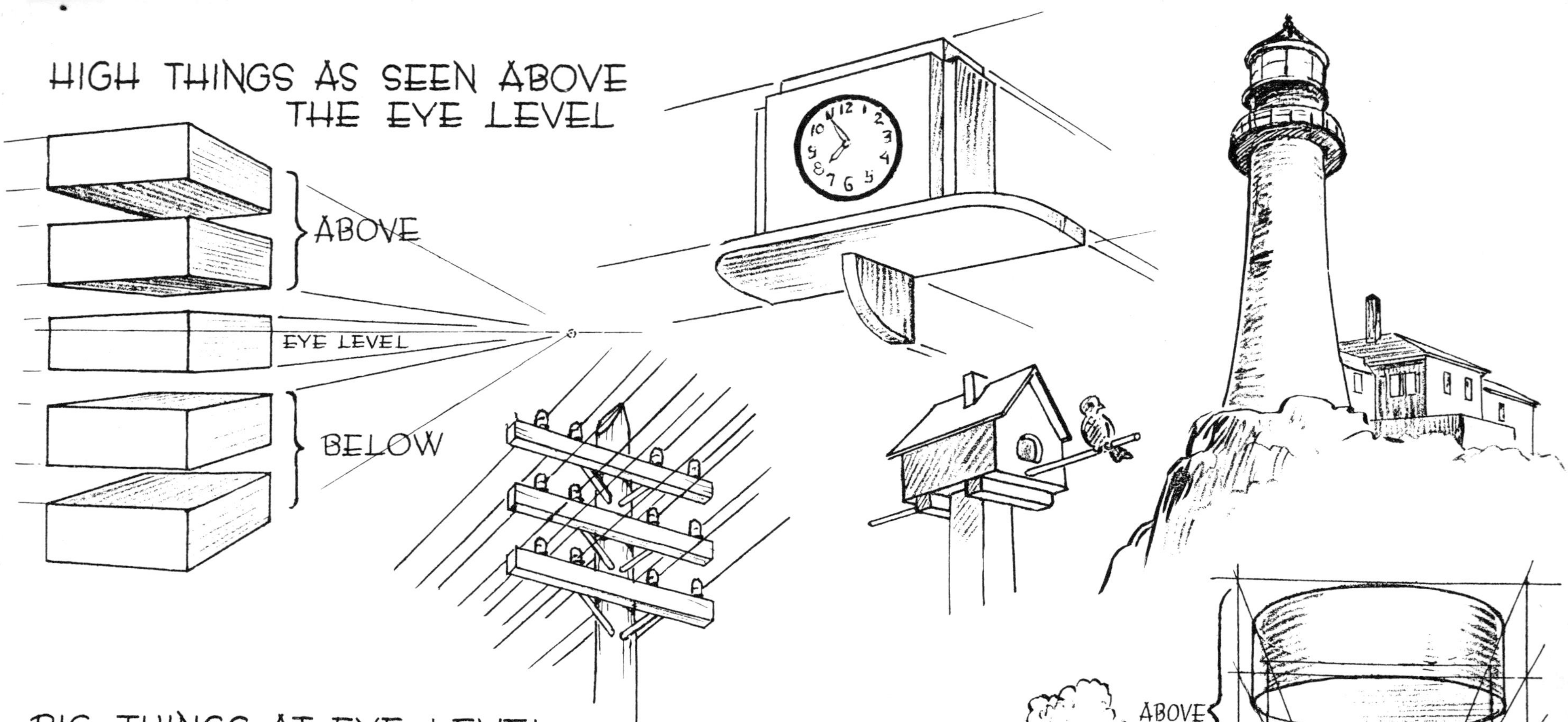

BIG THINGS AT EYE LEVEL

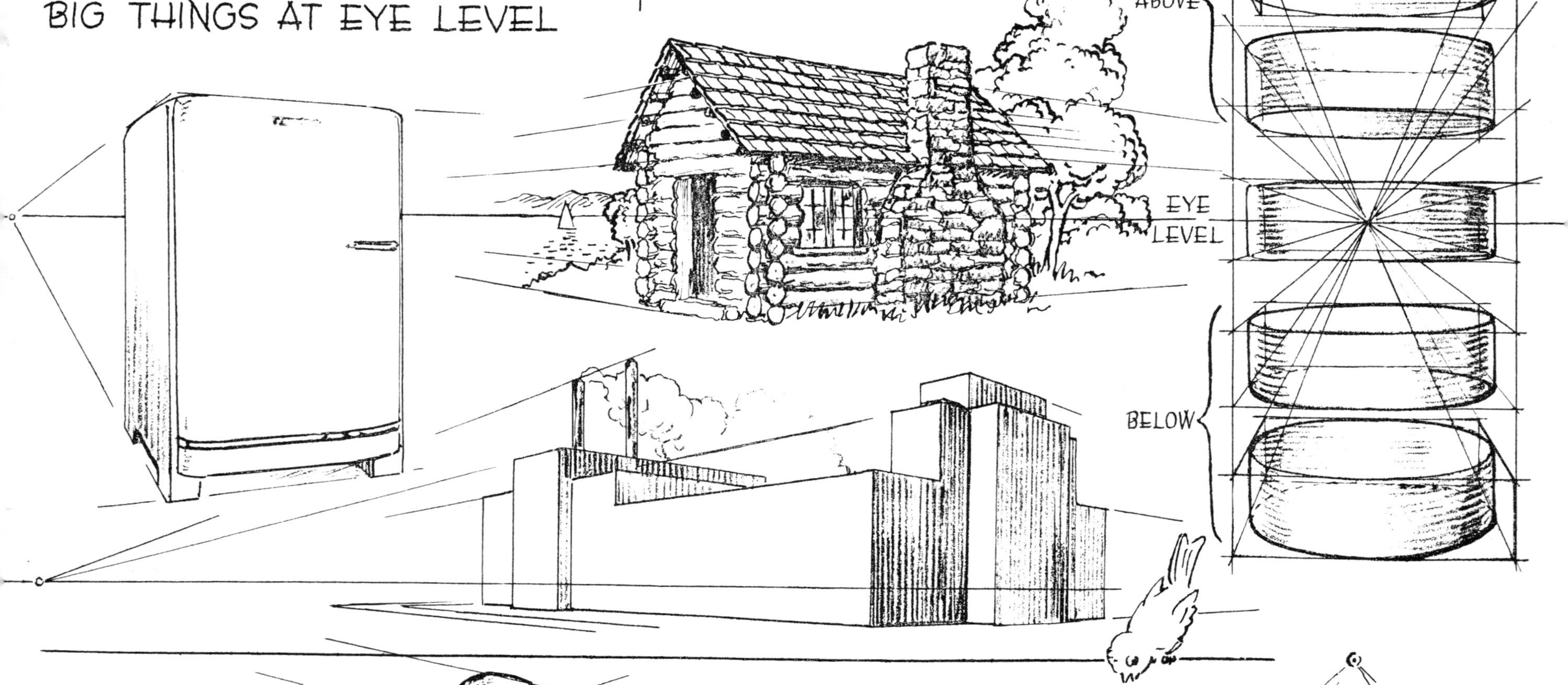

SMALL THINGS AS SEEN BELOW EYE LEVEL

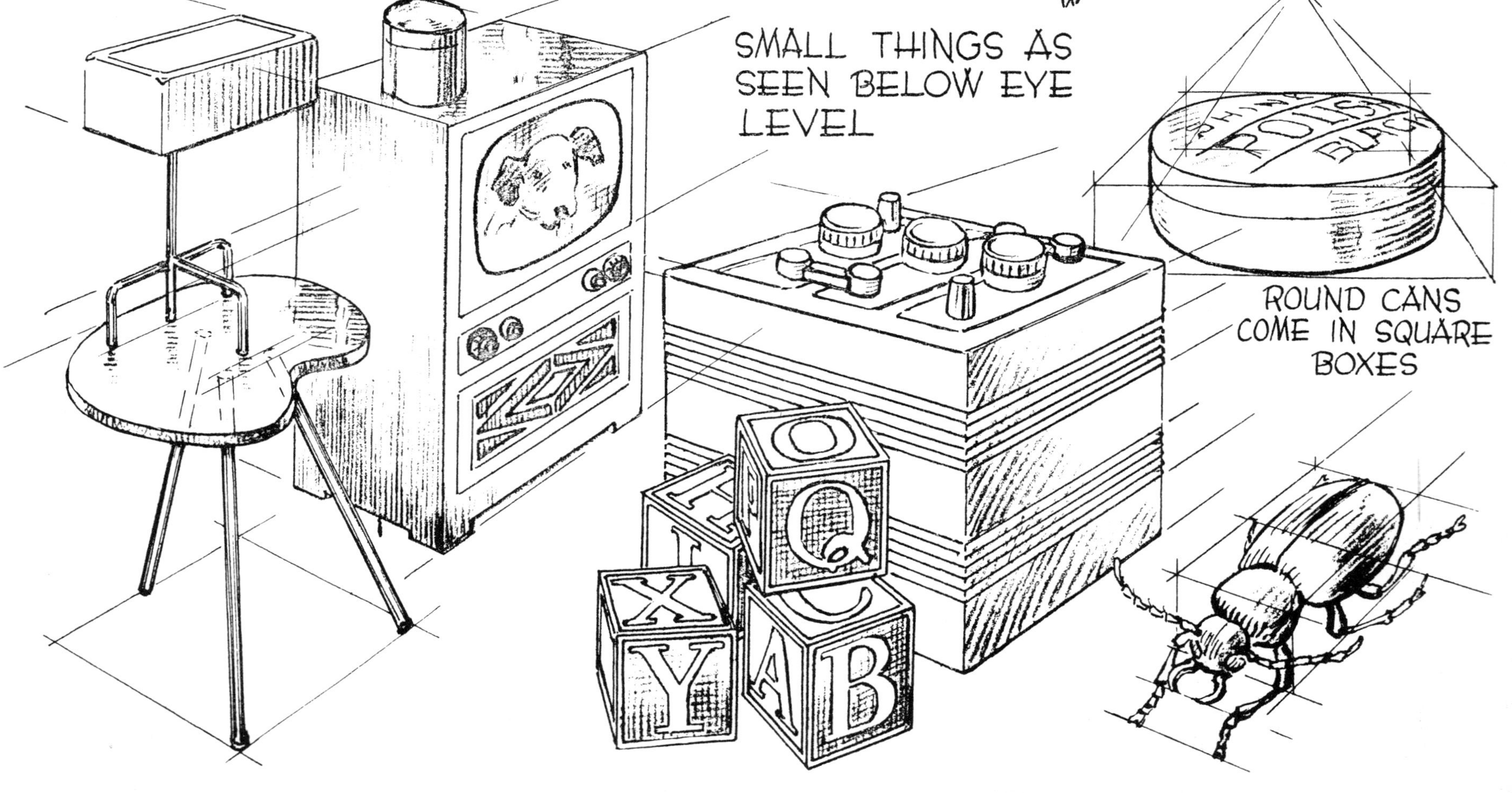

YOU CAN MAKE A PERSPECTIVE DRAWING OF YOUR OWN ROOM

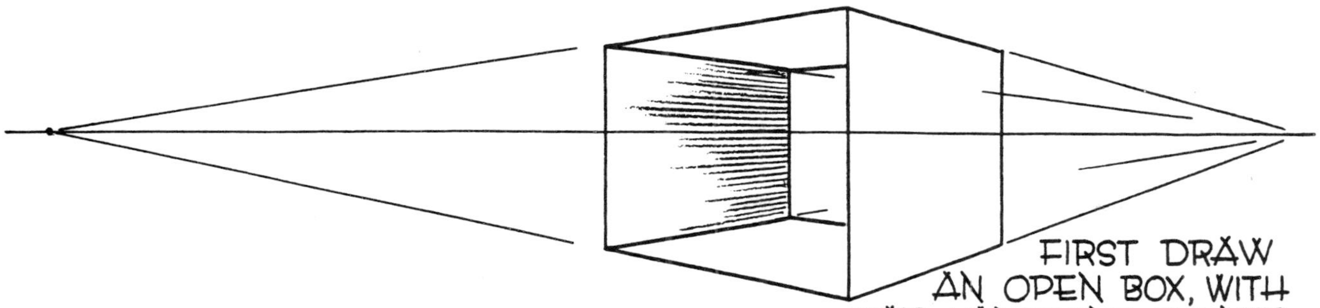

FIRST DRAW AN OPEN BOX, WITH TWO VANISHING POINTS ....EYE LEVEL

NEXT REMOVE THE SIDES NEAREST TO YOU—THIS LEAVES A CORNER IN YOUR ROOM.
(LET US DRAW IT LARGER)

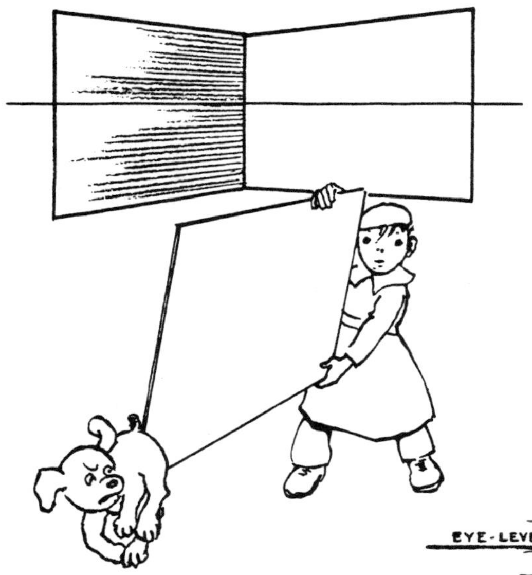

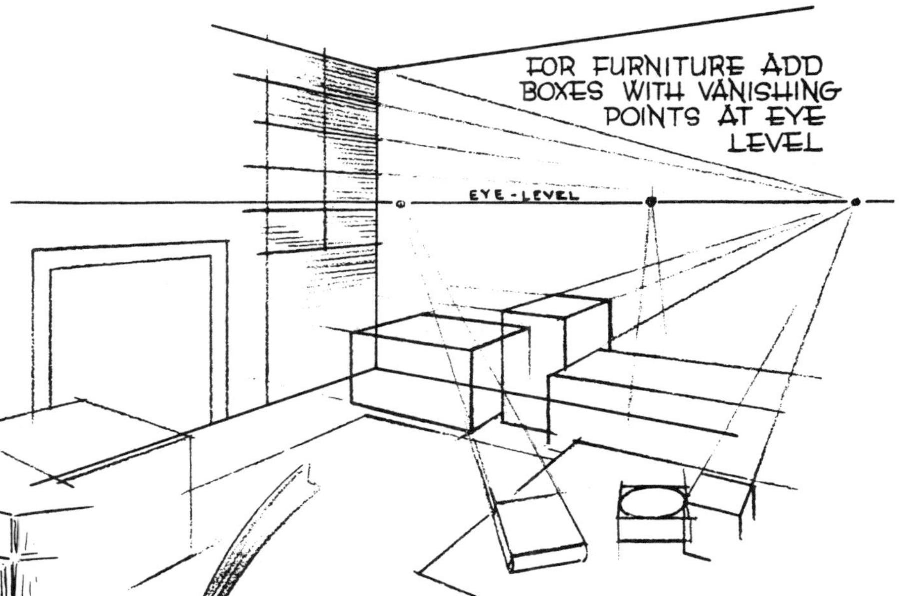

FOR FURNITURE ADD BOXES WITH VANISHING POINTS AT EYE LEVEL

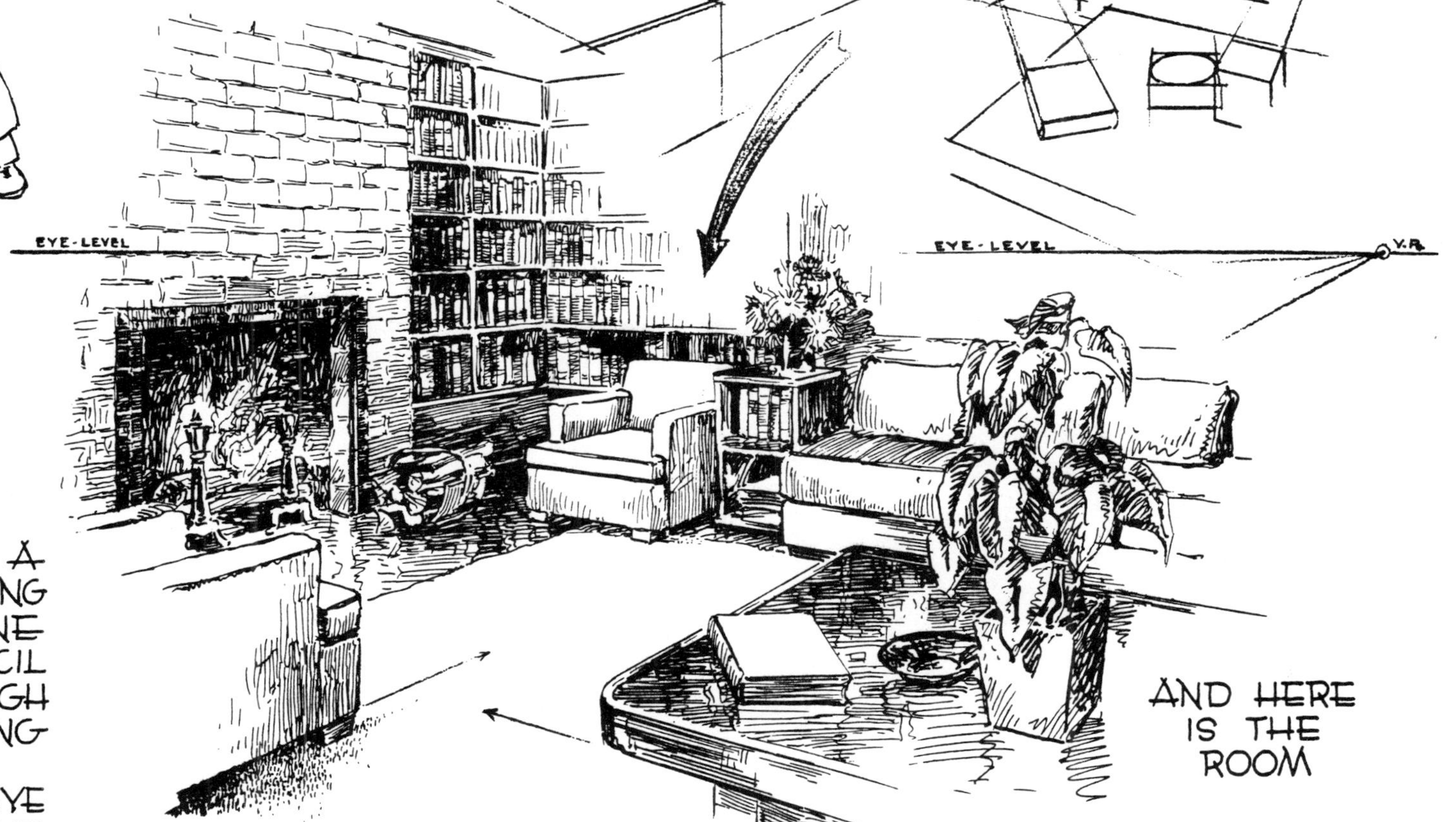

YOU CAN MAKE A PERSPECTIVE DRAWING ON A WINDOW PANE WITH A GREASE PENCIL BY LOOKING THROUGH A HOLE AND TRACING WHAT YOU SEE.
THE HOLE IS YOUR "EYE LEVEL" AND IT IS THE SAME HEIGHT AS THE "HORIZON LINE."

AND HERE IS THE ROOM

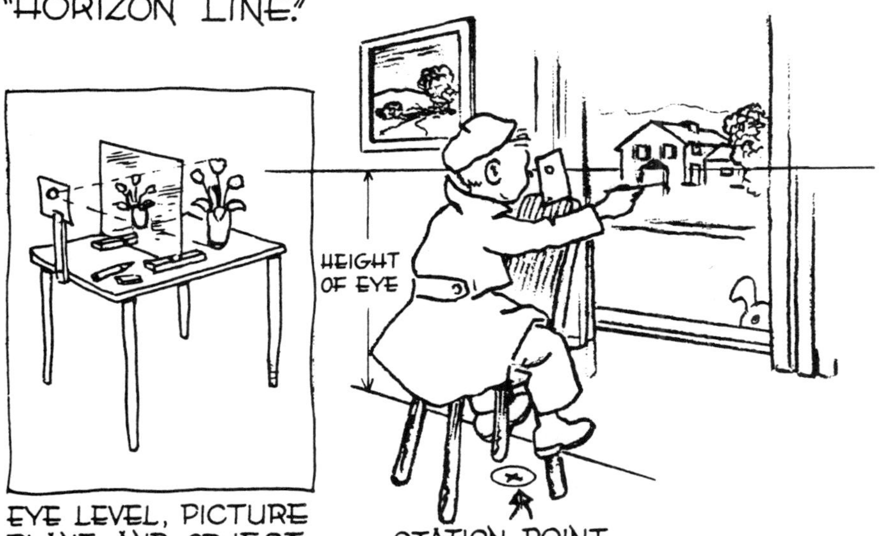

EYE LEVEL, PICTURE PLANE AND OBJECT

STATION POINT ON THE FLOOR

THE WINDOW PANE IS THE "PICTURE PLANE" AND THE SPOT ON THE FLOOR BELOW YOU IS YOUR "STATION POINT."

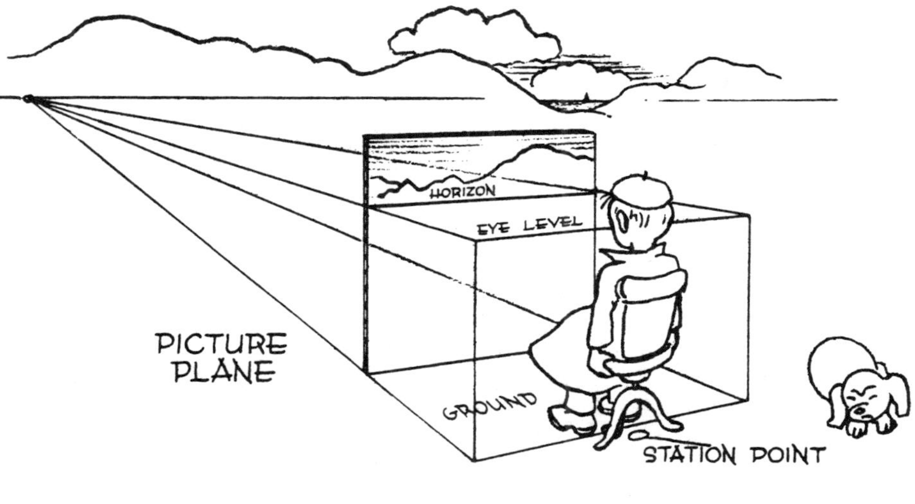

PICTURE PLANE

STATION POINT

BACK TO THE "OUTDOOR" ARTIST.
HE TOO HAS A PICTURE PLANE, A STATION POINT, A HORIZON AND EYE LEVEL

LOCATING THE VANISHING POINTS

THE VANISHING POINTS ARE SOMEWHERE ON THE HORIZON LINE – BUT WHERE?

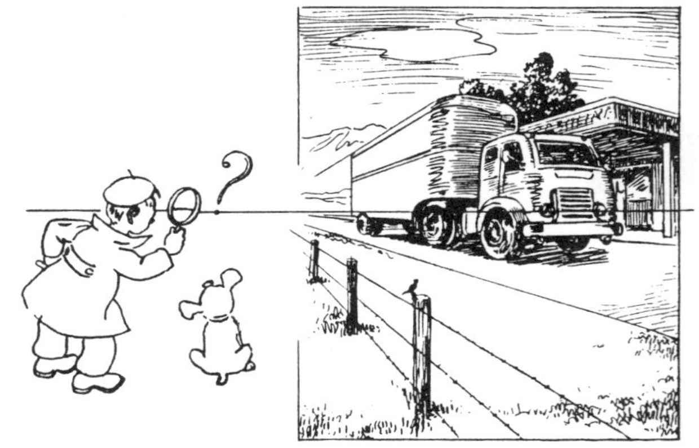

HERE IS THE ARTIST AGAIN DRAWING A BOX

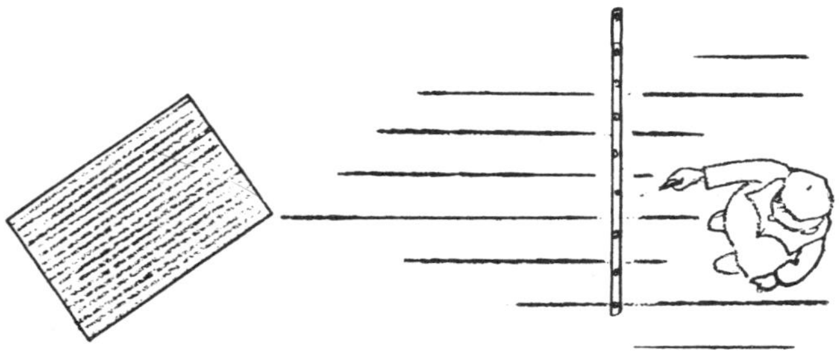

WE ARE LOOKING STRAIGHT DOWN ON HIM. HE IS STANDING ON HIS STATION POINT AND HE IS DRAWING ON A TRANSPARENT PICTURE PLANE. WE ARE LOOKING DOWN ON ITS TOP EDGE.

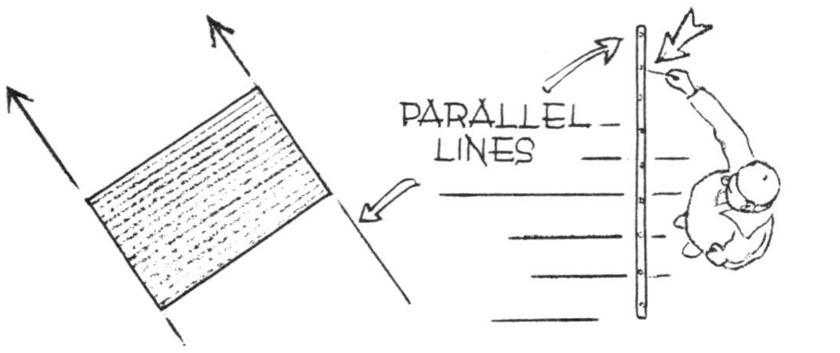

NOW IN ORDER TO FIND A VANISHING POINT ON HIS HORIZON LINE HE WILL HAVE TO LOOK IN THE DIRECTION PARALLEL TO THE SIDES OF THE BOX.

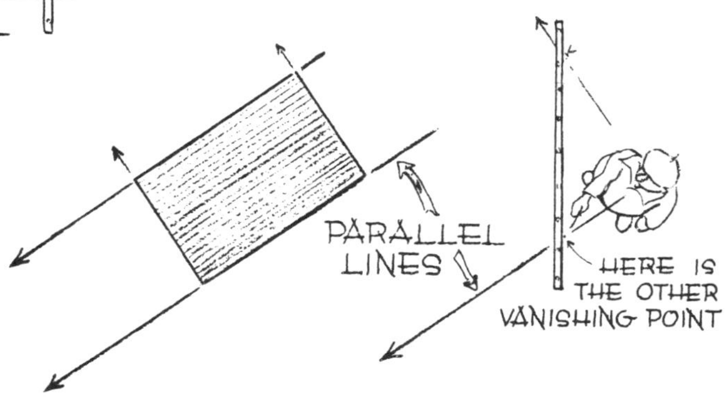

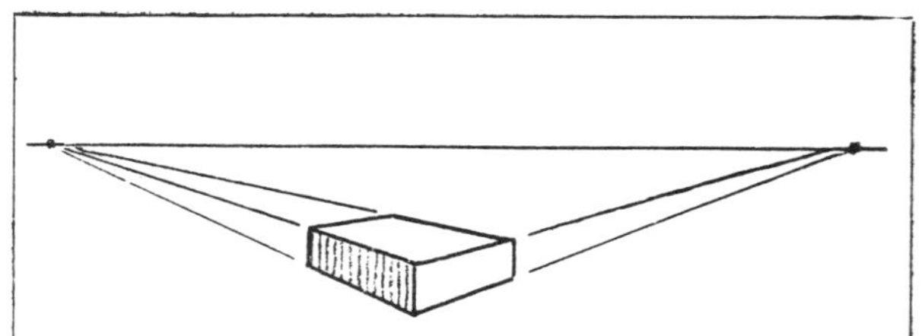

AND HERE IS THE DRAWING

AND SO WE FIND THE VANISHING POINTS SIMPLY BY POINTING IN THE SAME DIRECTION AS THE SIDES OF THE BOX.

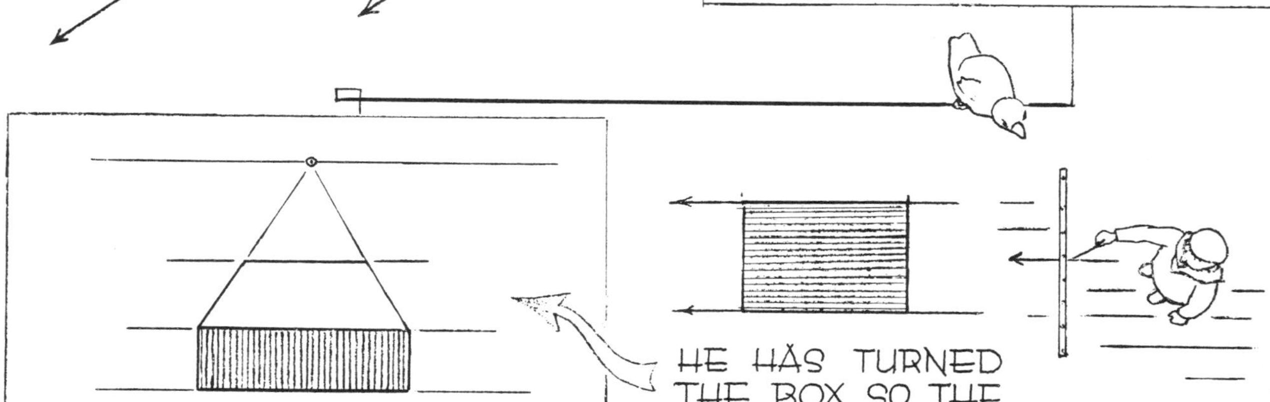

THE DRAWING, USING ONE VANISHING POINT

HE HAS TURNED THE BOX SO THE VANISHING POINT IS STRAIGHT AHEAD

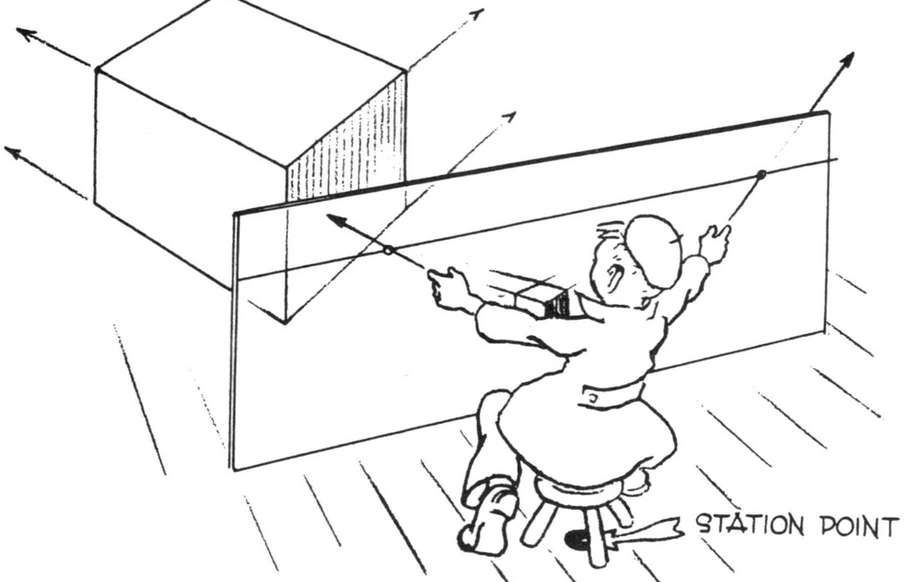

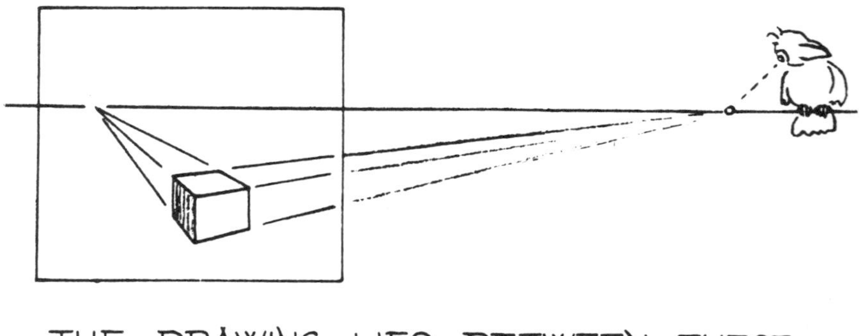

THE DRAWING LIES BETWEEN THESE TWO POINTS ON THE PICTURE PLANE.

VANISHING POINTS SHOULD BE PLACED FAR APART—LIKE THIS

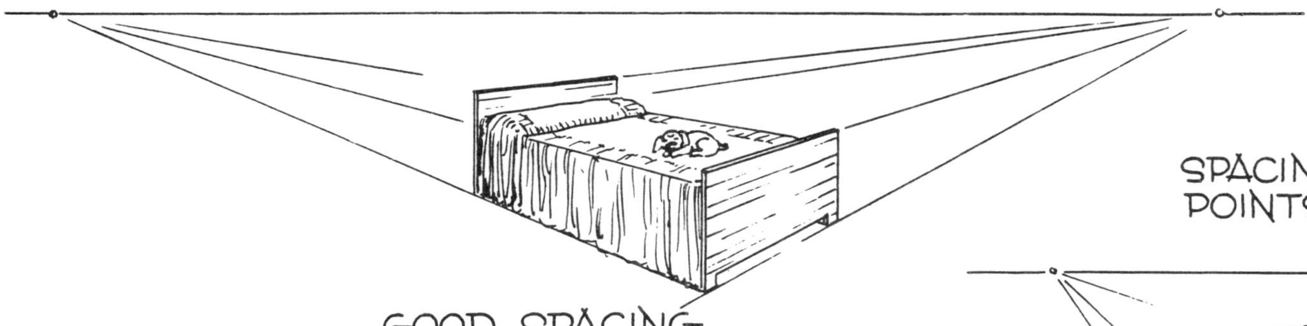

GOOD SPACING

SPACING WITH VANISHING POINTS TOO CLOSE

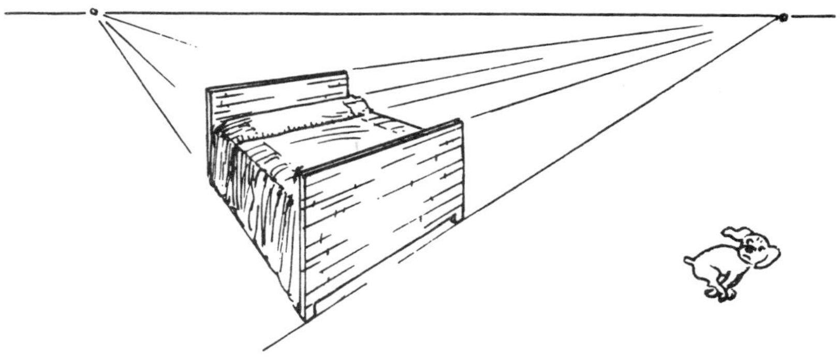

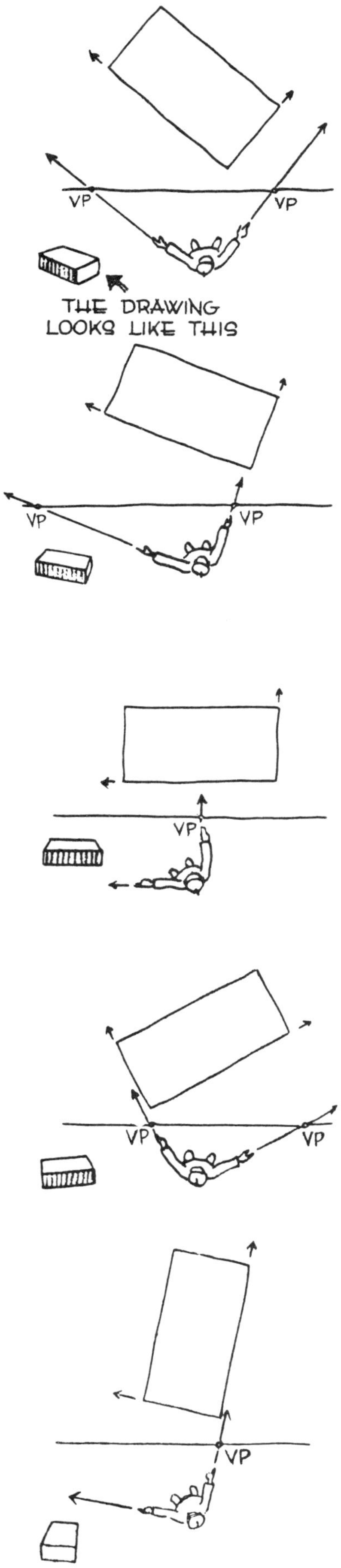

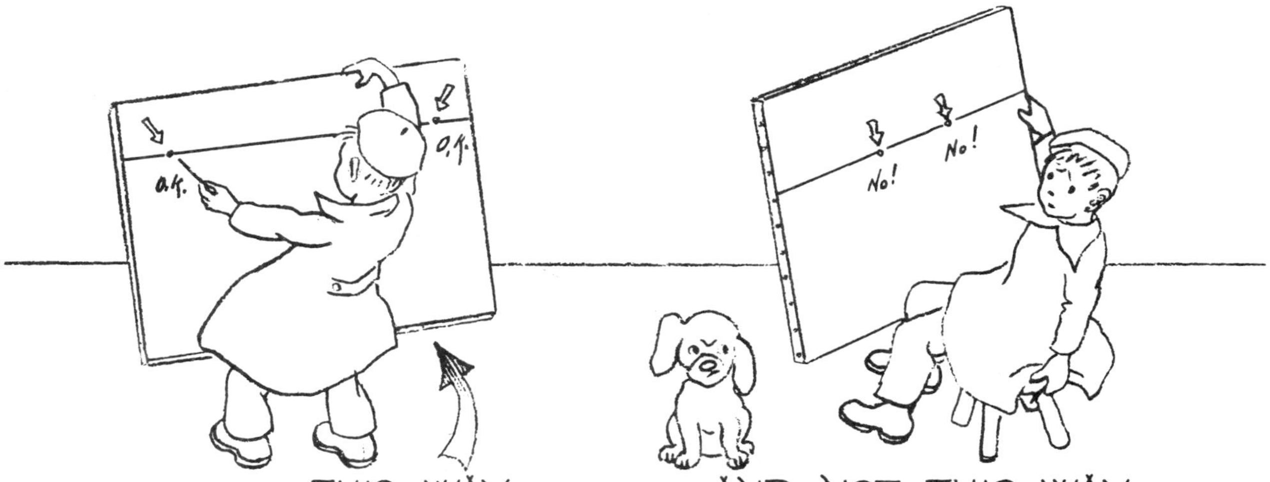

THIS WAY —— AND NOT THIS WAY

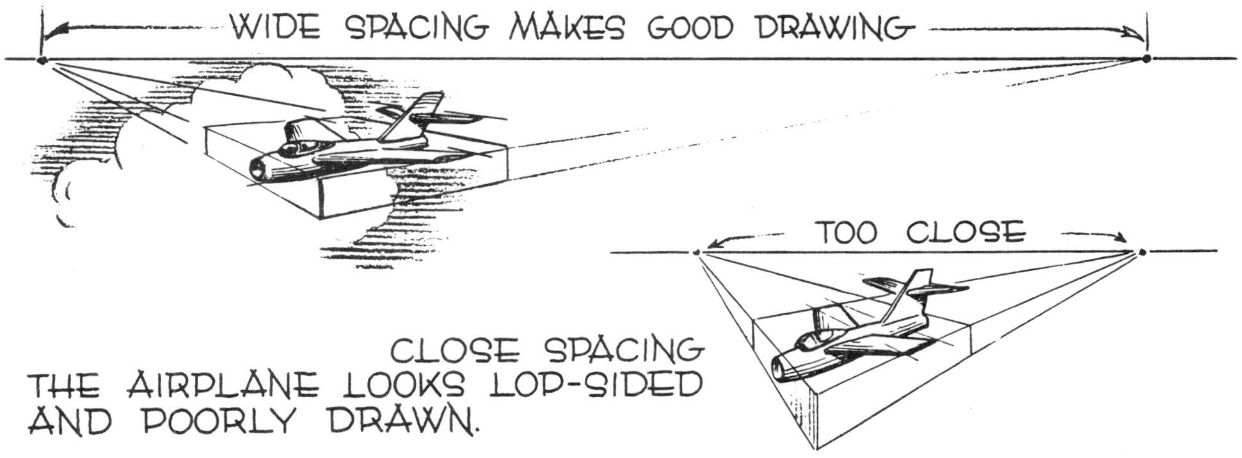

CLOSE SPACING
THE AIRPLANE LOOKS LOP-SIDED AND POORLY DRAWN.

OFTEN WE FIND THAT ONE OF THE VANISHING POINTS IS CLEAR OFF THE DRAWING BOARD. A LONG RULER AND A PIN WILL BE A GREAT HELP.

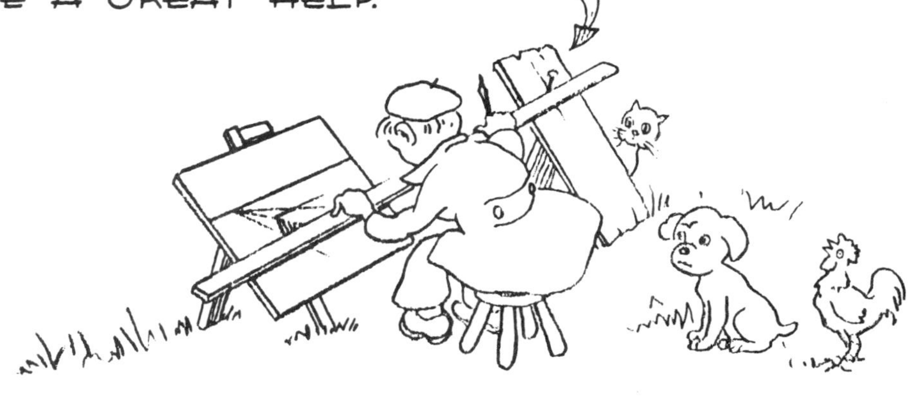

WE ARE READY TO MAKE A TRUE PERSPECTIVE DRAWING

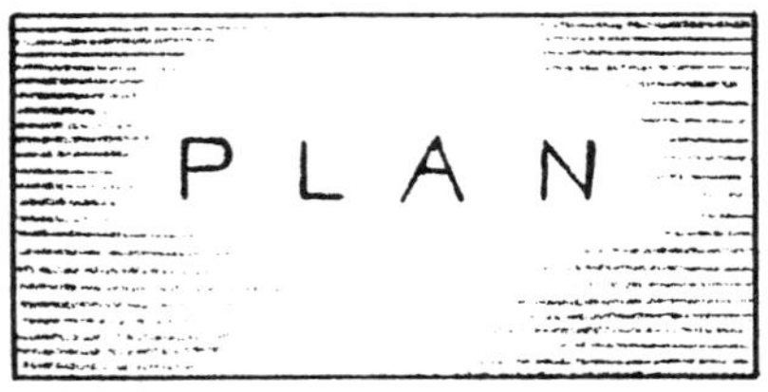

THIS IS THE TOP VIEW (THE PLAN) OF A BOX.

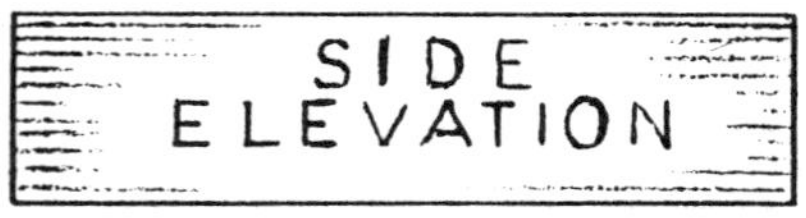

THIS IS THE SIDE VIEW (THE SIDE ELEVATION) OF THE SAME BOX.

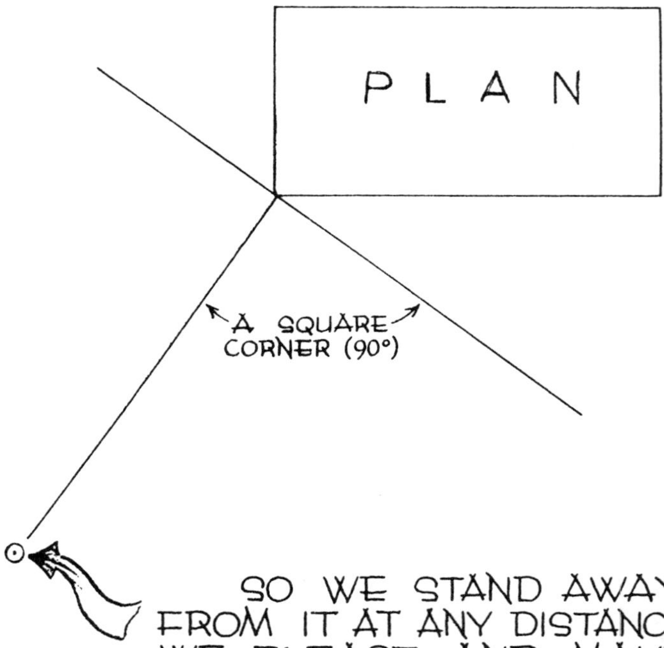

WE WISH TO MAKE A DRAWING OF THE BOX— LOOKING AT IT CORNERWISE.

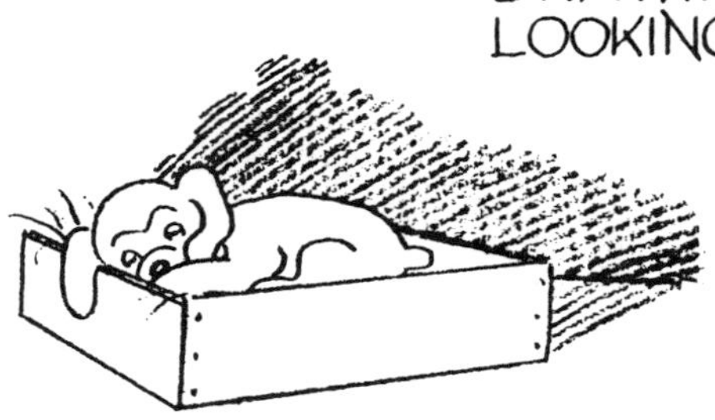

SO WE STAND AWAY FROM IT AT ANY DISTANCE WE PLEASE AND MAKE A DOT AT OUR STATION POINT.

NOW WE DRAW THE LINE WHICH REPRESENTS THE PICTURE PLANE RESTING UPRIGHT AGAINST THE CORNER OF THE PLAN LIKE THIS!

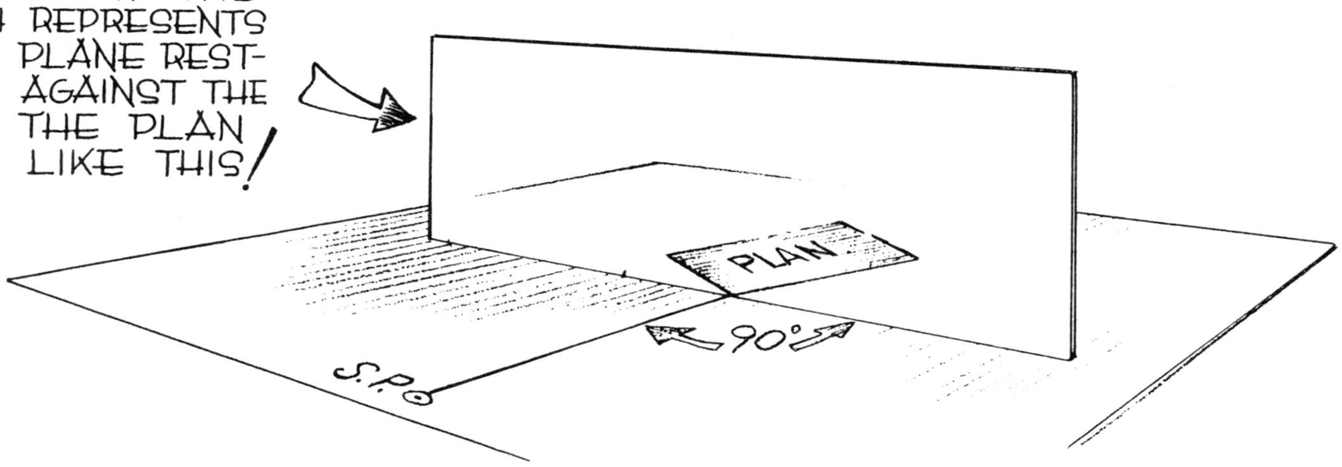

IF THE BOX COULD BE PLACED ON THE PLAN IT WOULD LOOK LIKE THIS. WE WOULD LOOK AT IT FROM A POSITION DIRECTLY ABOVE THE STATION POINT AT ANY CONVENIENT HEIGHT.

(THE HEAVY BLACK LINE AT THE CORNER OF THE BOX IS ITS TRUE HEIGHT ON THE PICTURE PLANE.)

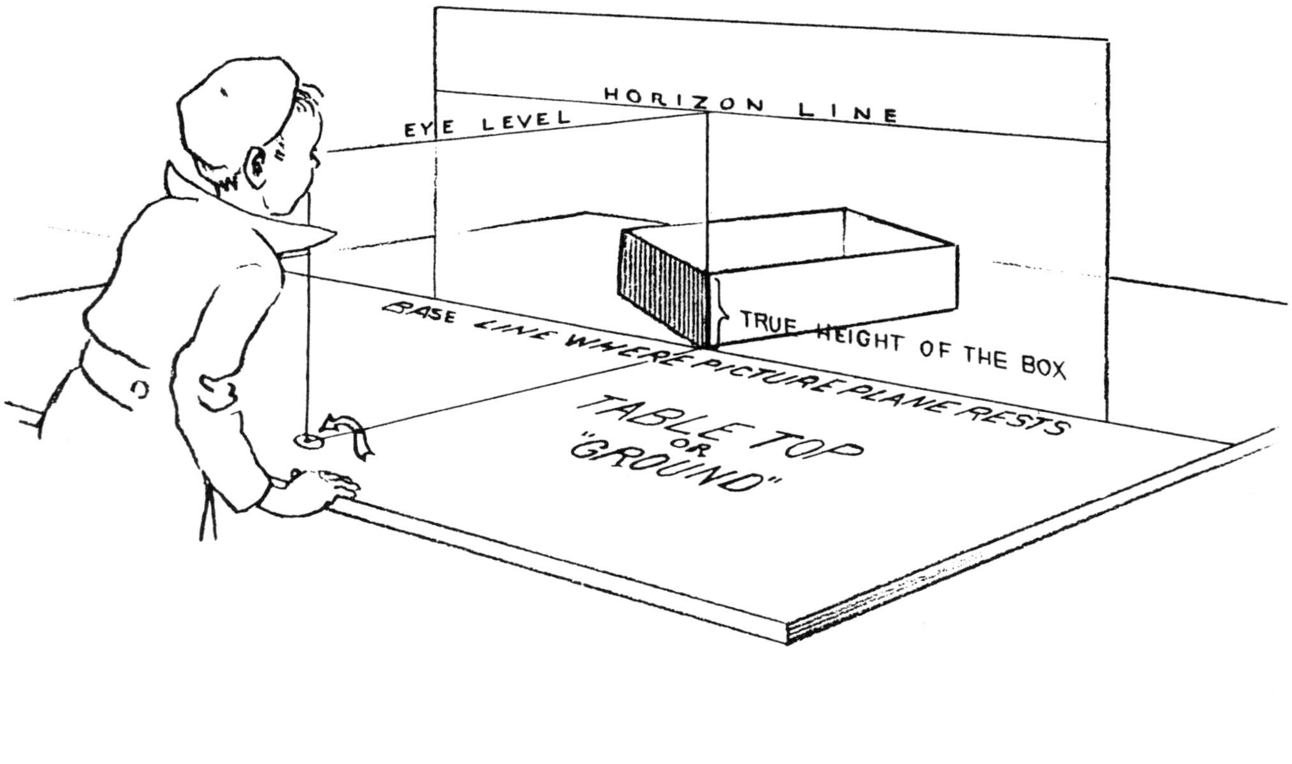

WE LOCATE THE VANISHING POINTS BY RUNNING LINES FROM THE EYE TO THE PICTURE PLANE, PARALLEL TO THE SIDES OF THE BOX.

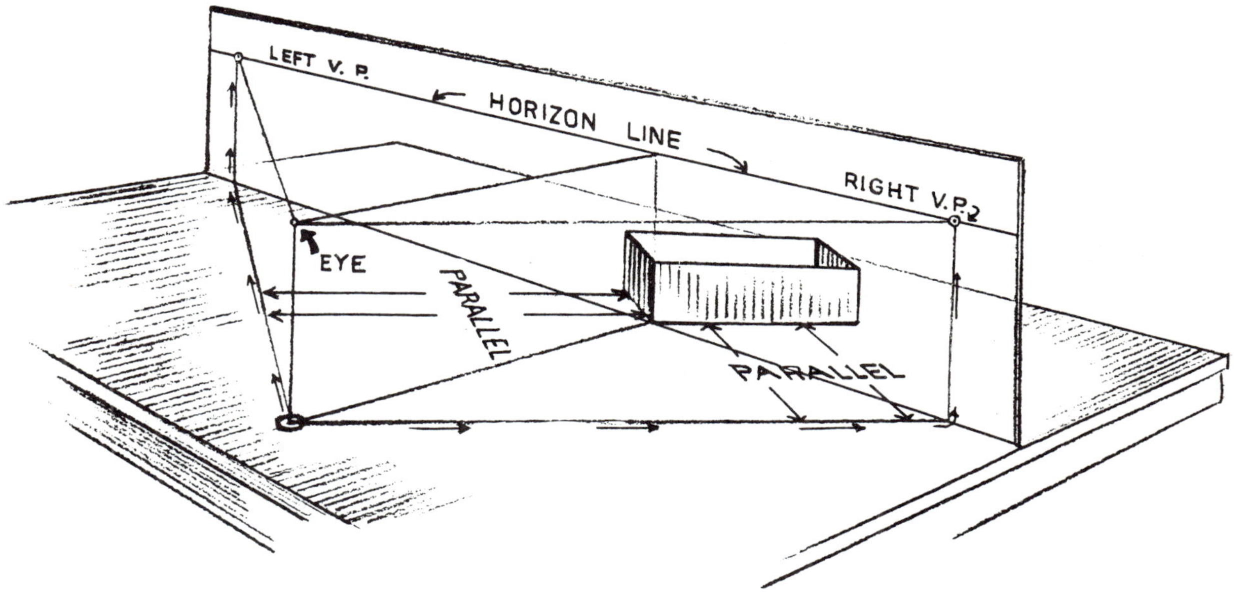

WE ARE MAKING THE DRAWING ON THE PICTURE PLANE. WE WANT IT FOR CONVENIENCE TO LIE FLAT ON THE TABLE TOP, OR GROUND. TO DO THIS WE SLIDE IT —— AS SHOWN —— TOWARDS US INTO THE OPEN SPACE BETWEEN THE STATION POINT AND THE PLAN.

VANISHING POINTS COME FORWARD TOO.

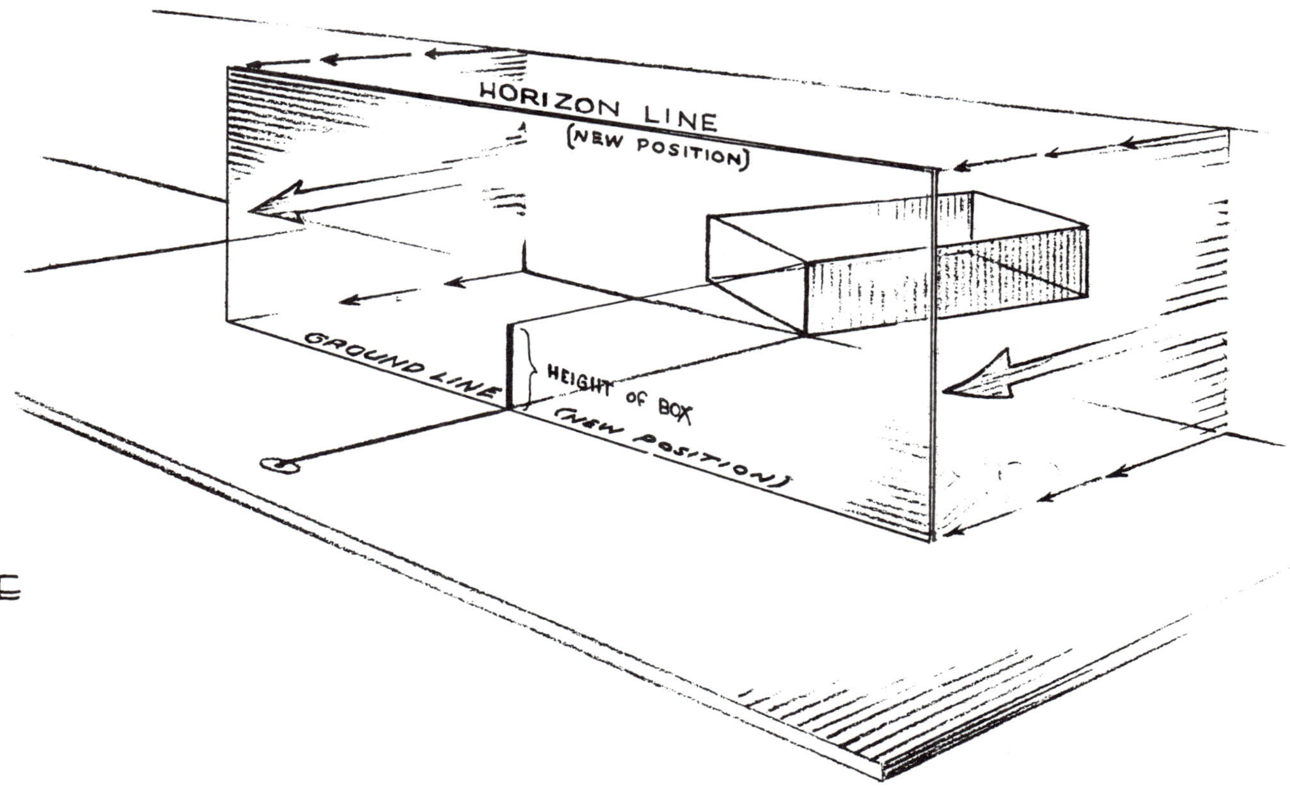

WE LOCATE THE VANISHING POINTS BY RUNNING LINES FROM THE EYE TO THE PICTURE PLANE, PARALLEL TO THE SIDES OF THE BOX.

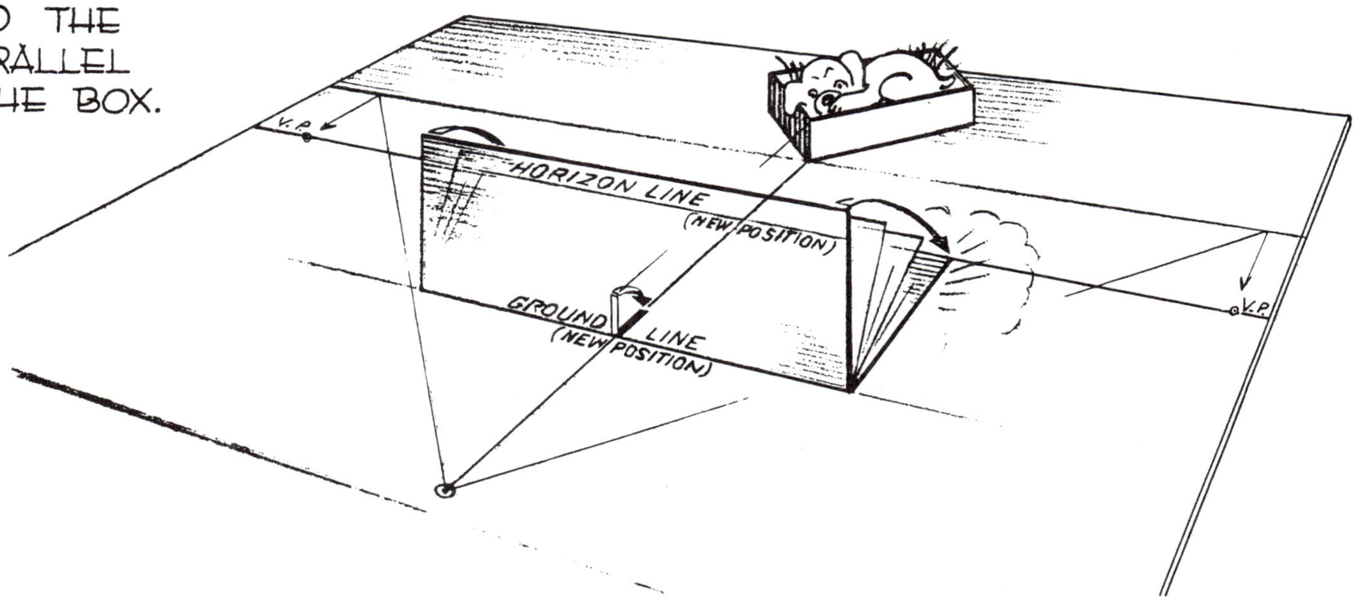

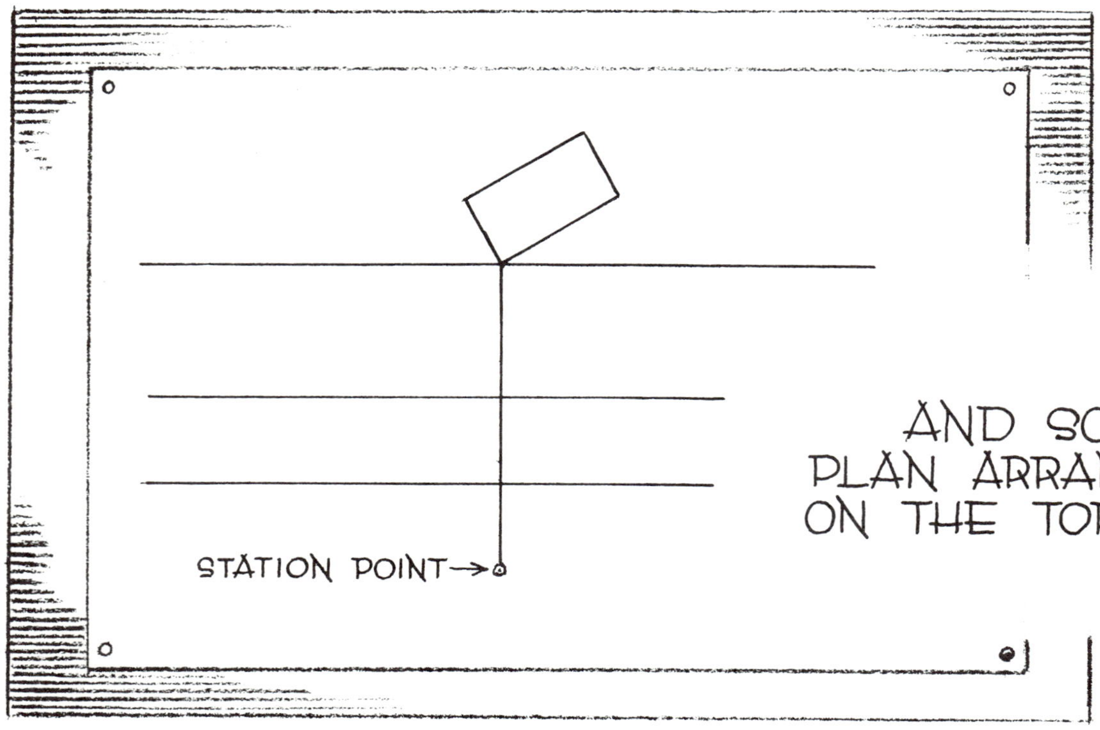

AND SO WE HAVE THE PLAN ARRANGED LIKE THIS ON THE TOP OF THE TABLE.

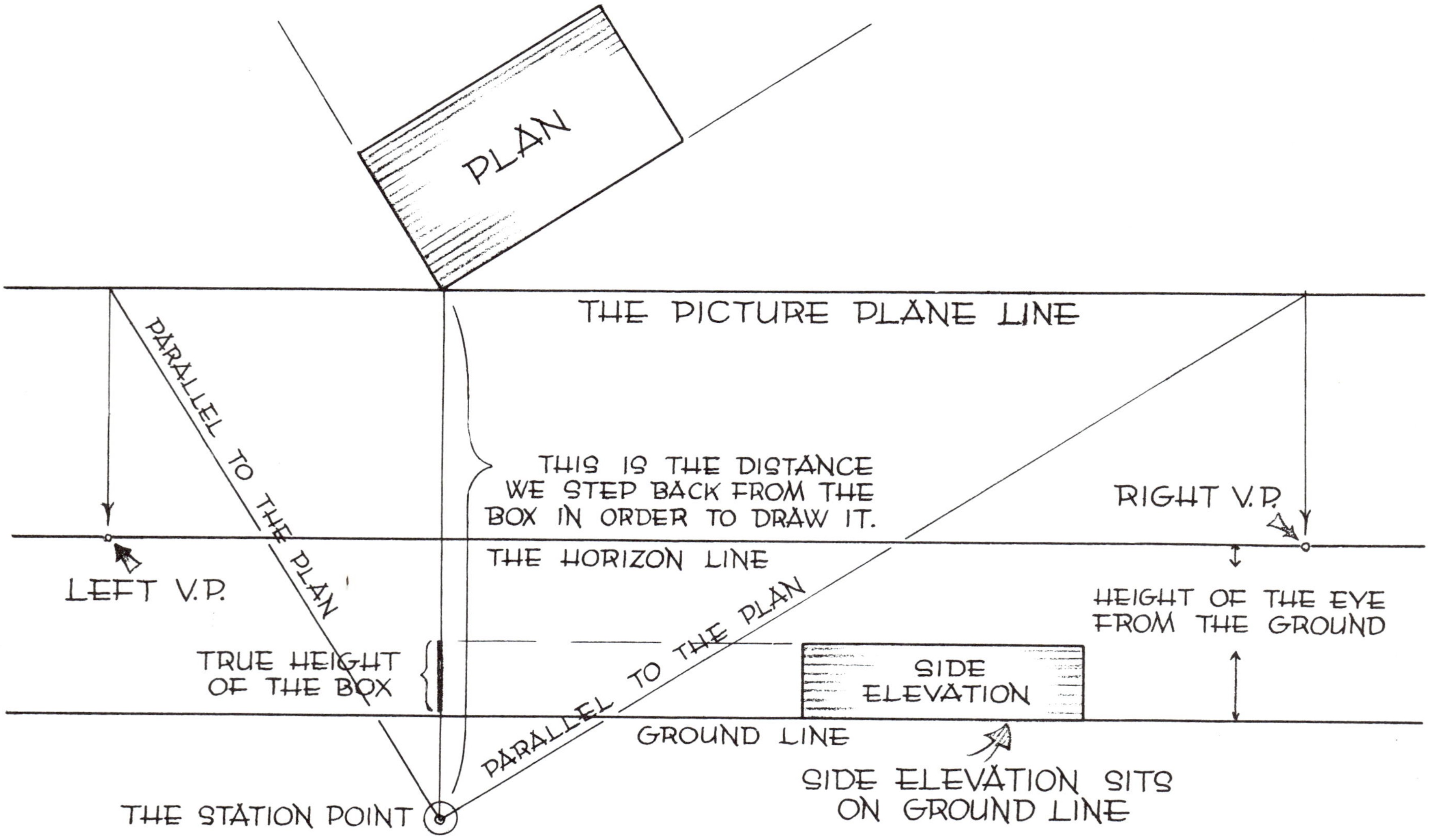

HERE IS THE TYPICAL PERSPECTIVE PLAN WITH THE PARTS NAMED.

NOTICE THAT THE VANISHING POINTS ARE TRANSFERRED TO THE HORIZON LINE WHICH IS NOW LYING ON THE GROUND. THEIR DISTANCE APART REMAINS UNCHANGED.

THE DRAWING OF THE SIDE ELEVATION IS PLACED ON THE GROUND LINE. HERE IT IS USED FOR THE UP AND DOWN OR HEIGHT MEASUREMENTS.

HERE'S AN EASY WAY TO REMEMBER THE LAYOUT FOR A PERSPECTIVE DRAWING

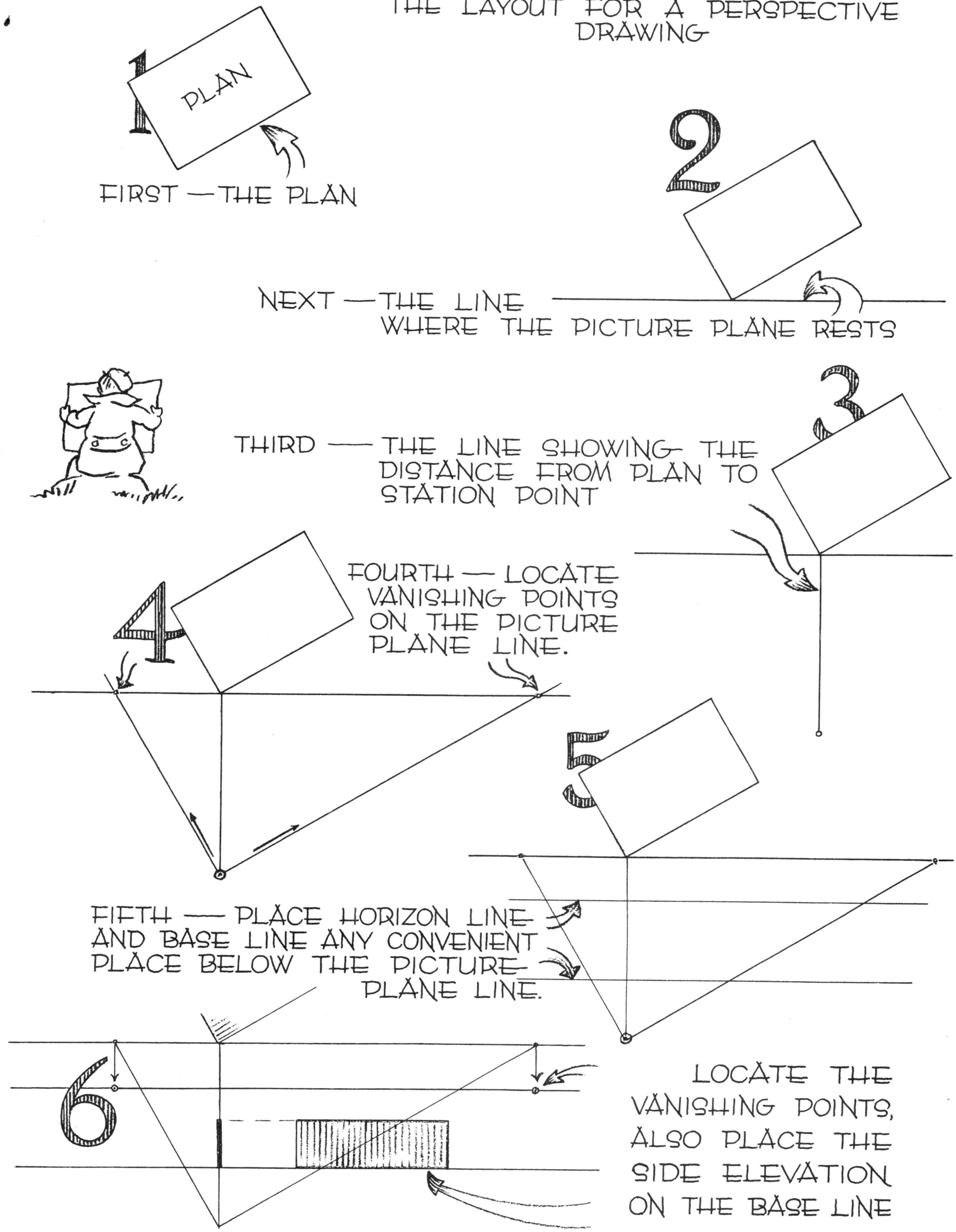

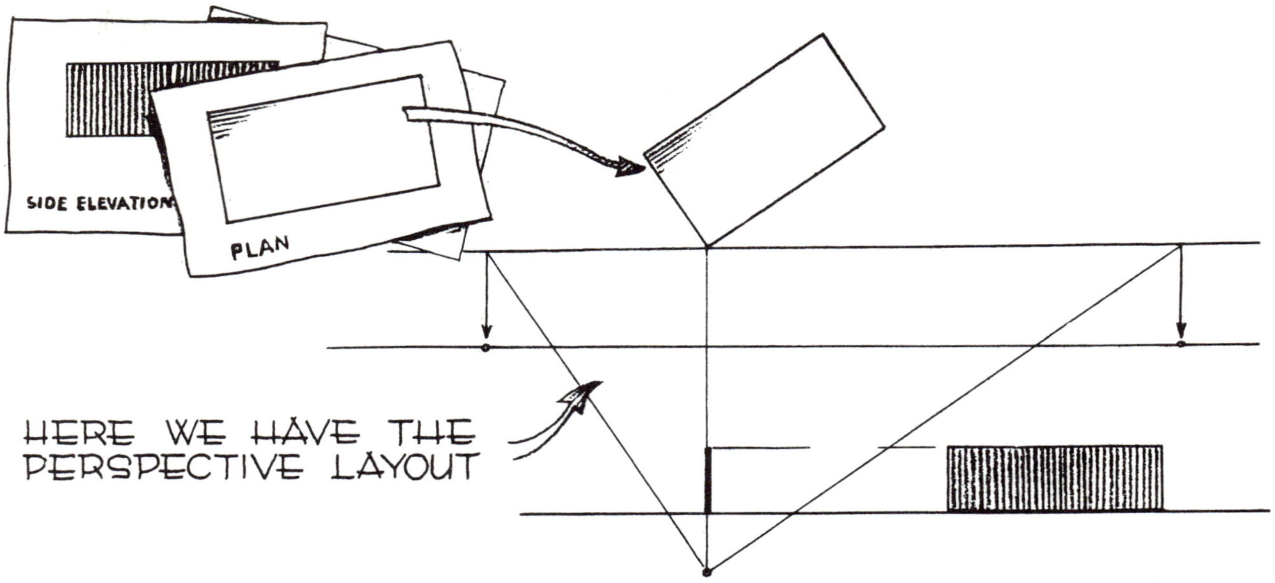

HERE WE HAVE THE PERSPECTIVE LAYOUT

WE ARE NOW READY FOR THE PROJECTION

THE WALL, LIKE THE RAILROAD TRACK, DISAPPEARS AT THE VANISHING POINTS ON THE HORIZON. THE WALL IS THE HEIGHT OF THE BOX; — IT IS MADE BY DRAWING FOUR LINES FROM THE TOP AND BOTTOM OF THE HEAVY LINE OUT TO THE VANISHING POINTS. NOW ALL WE HAVE TO DO IS TO CUT THE TWO WALLS OFF AT THE PROPER LENGTH SO AS TO MAKE TWO SIDES OF THE BOX.

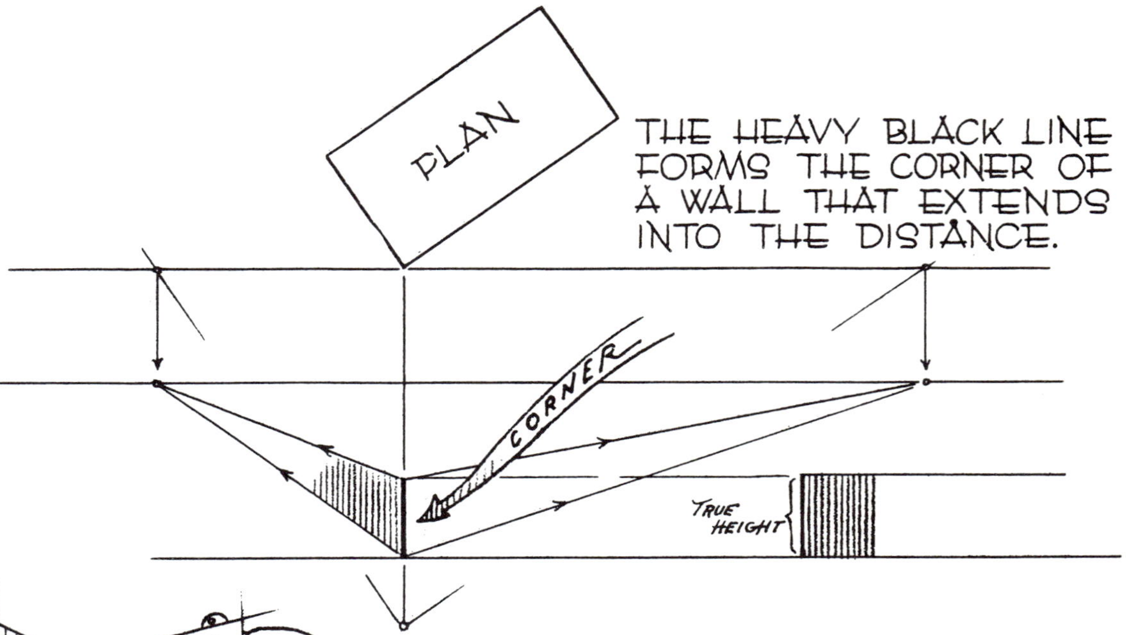

THE HEAVY BLACK LINE FORMS THE CORNER OF A WALL THAT EXTENDS INTO THE DISTANCE.

LET'S SEE HOW IT'S DONE

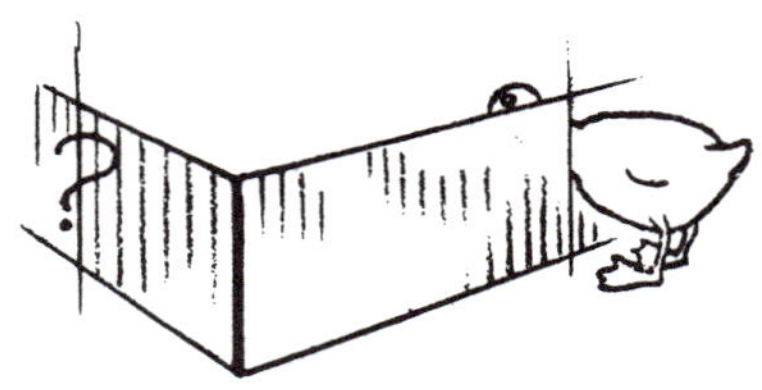

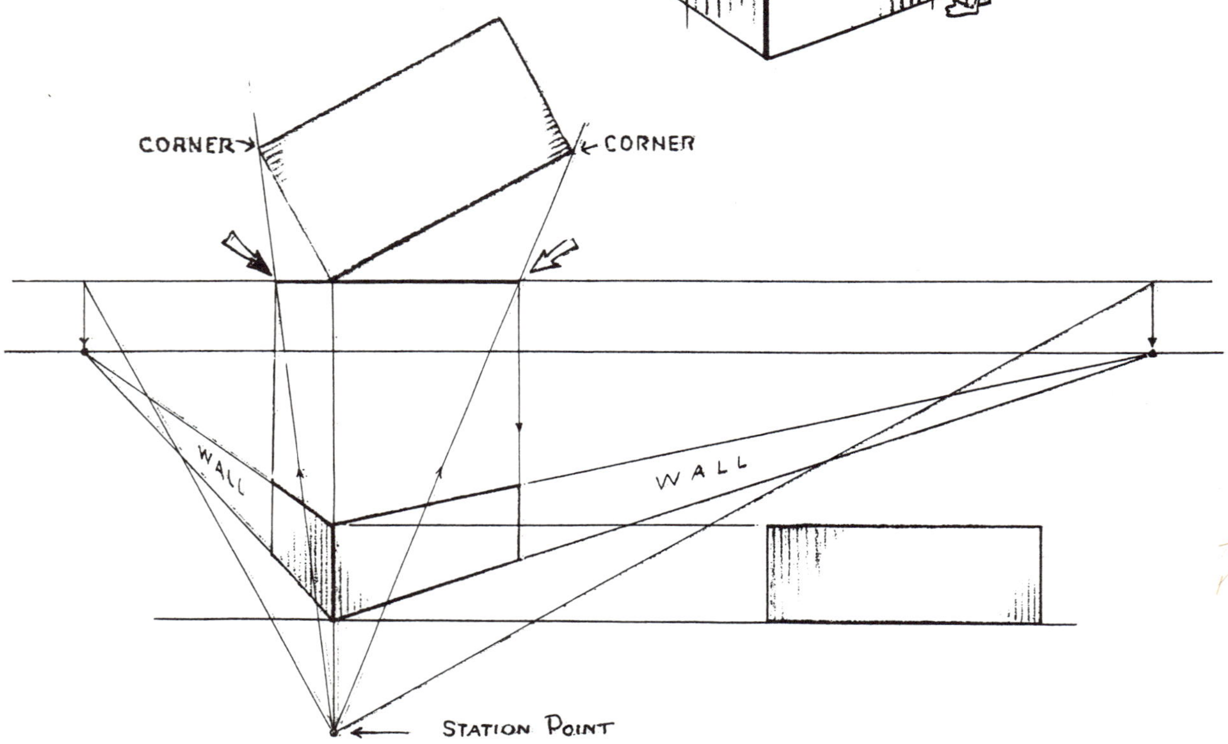

WE ARE STANDING AT THE STATION POINT LOOKING AT THE PLAN. FROM HERE WE LOOK ALONG A STRAIGHT LINE TO A POINT AT THE CORNER OF THE PLAN. THIS LINE PASSES THROUGH THE PICTURE PLANE AT THE POINT INDICATED BY THE ARROW. THERE ARE TWO OF THESE POINTS, ONE FOR EACH CORNER.

NOW THE BOX AS WE SEE IT ON THE PICTURE PLANE LIES IN THE SPACE BETWEEN THE ARROWS. IT IS NO WIDER THAN THIS SPACE. SO LINES FROM THE POINTS, DRAWN STRAIGHT DOWN, CUT THE WALLS OFF AT THE RIGHT WIDTH. WE NOW HAVE TWO SIDES OF THE BOX DRAWN IN PERSPECTIVE.

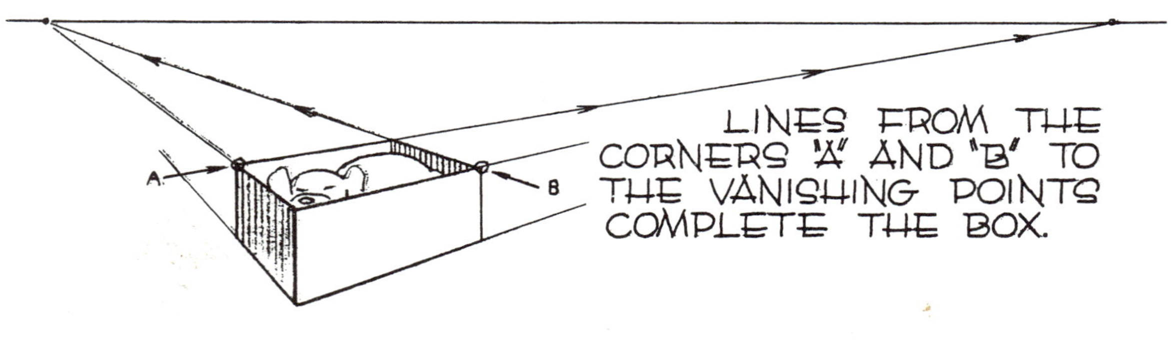

LINES FROM THE CORNERS "A" AND "B" TO THE VANISHING POINTS COMPLETE THE BOX.

NOW WE CAN MAKE A PERSPECTIVE DRAWING OF A HOUSE FROM A PLAN AND ELEVATION.

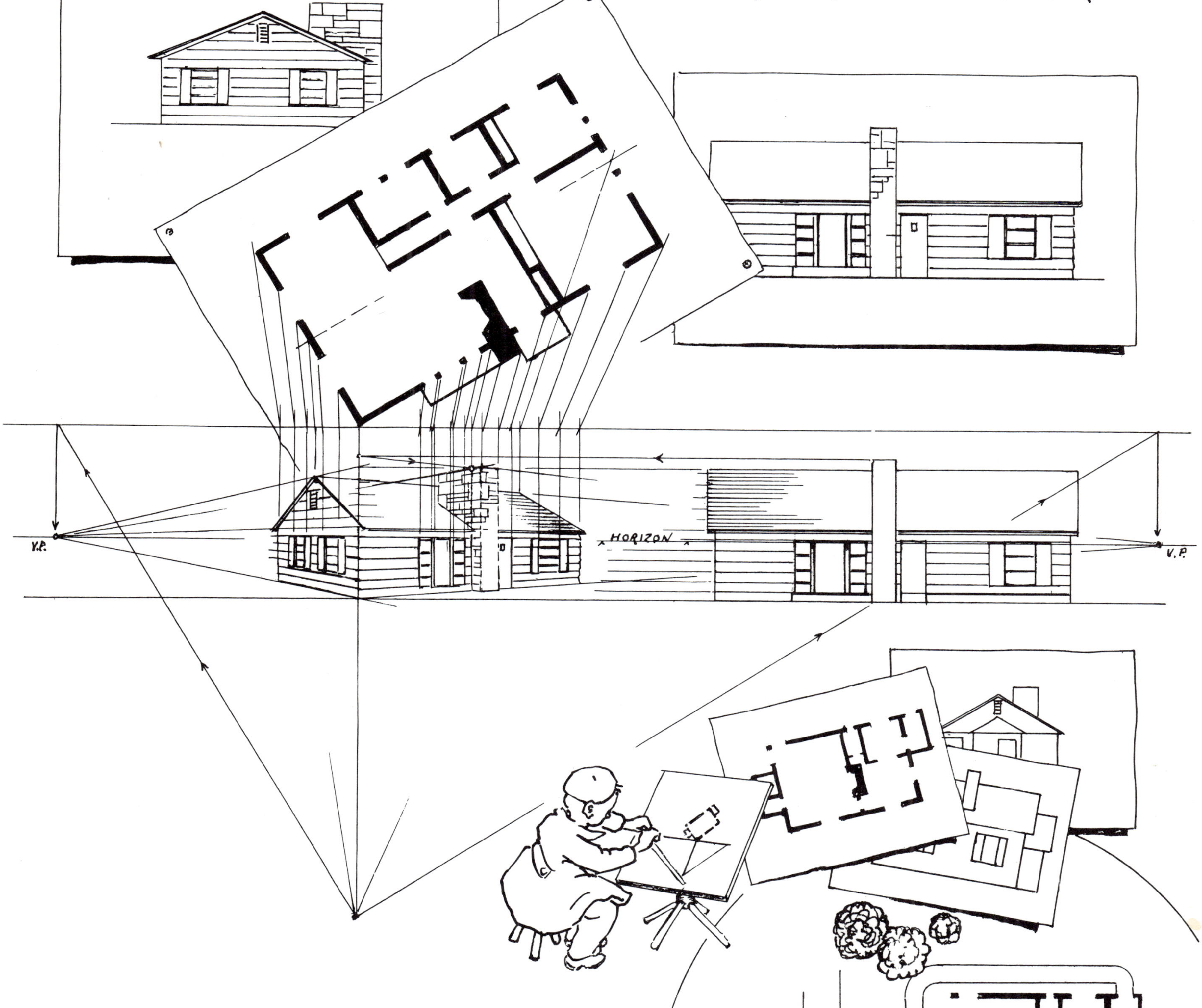

YOU CAN NOW MAKE A PERSPECTIVE DRAWING OF YOUR OWN HOME FROM THE BLUE-PRINTS AND FROM ANY VIEWPOINT

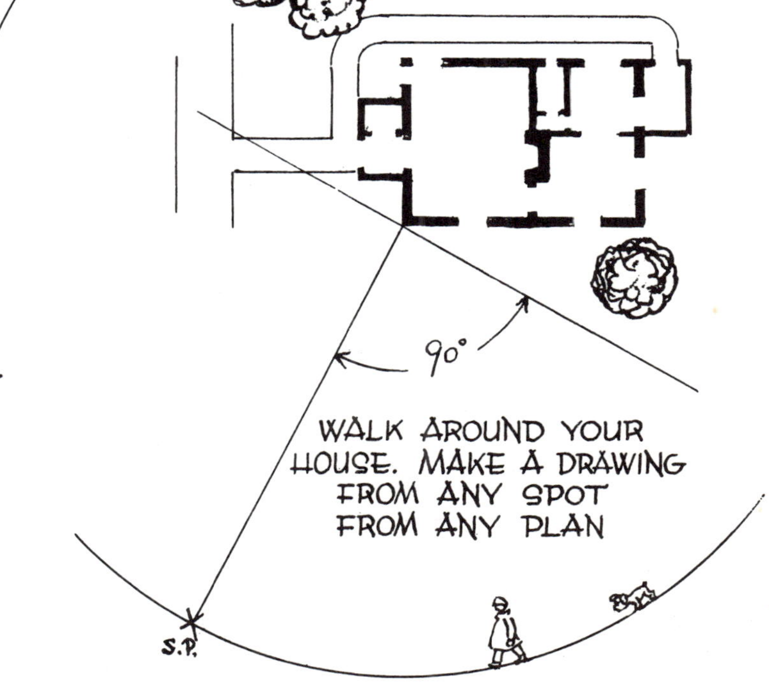

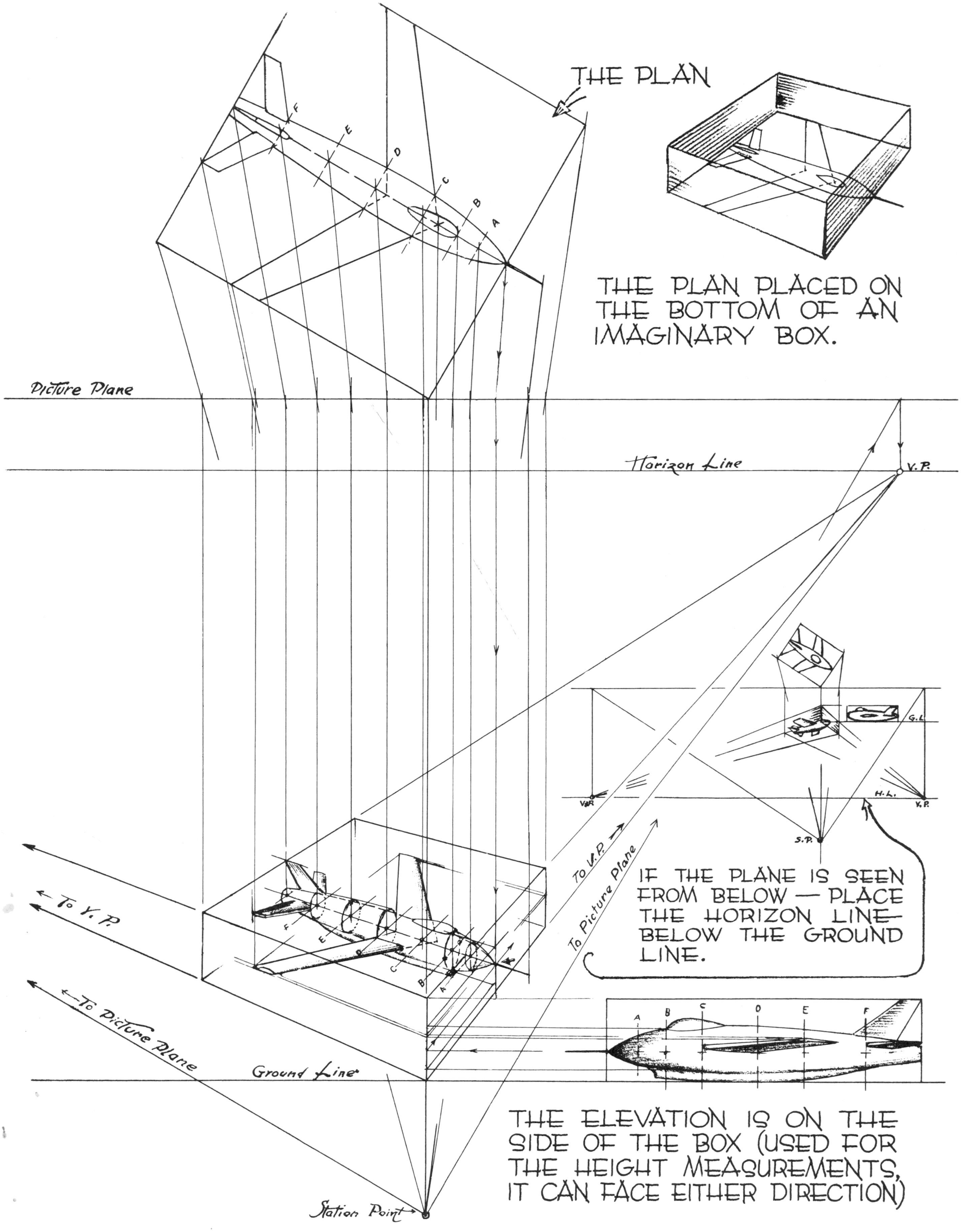

A PERSPECTIVE PROJECTION OF A JET PLANE DRAWN FROM A PLAN AND A SIDE ELEVATION

ANOTHER METHOD!

FIRST—STAND BACK AND LOOK AT THE HOUSE FROM THE VIEWPOINT S.P. DRAW THE PERSPECTIVE TRIANGLE.

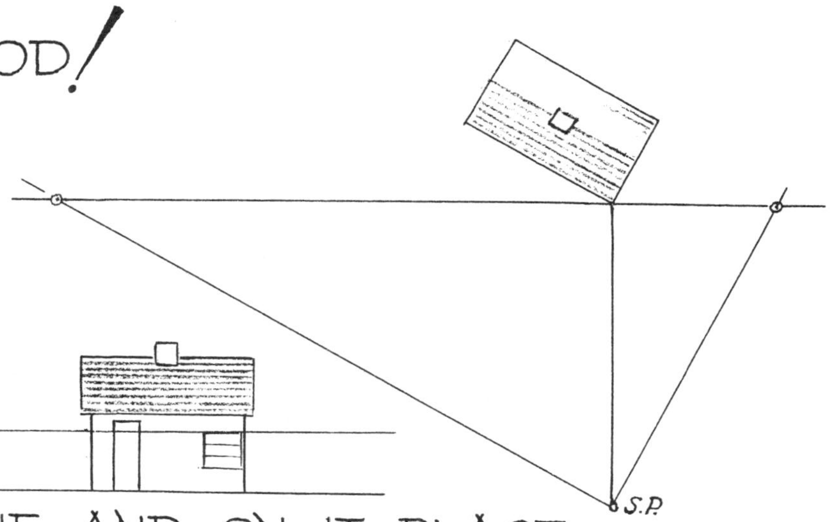

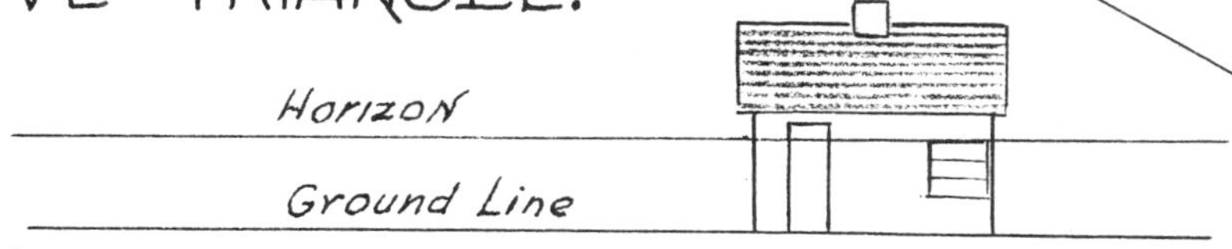

NEXT—DRAW A GROUND LINE AND ON IT PLACE THE "SIDE ELEVATION". PUT IN THE HORIZON LINE.

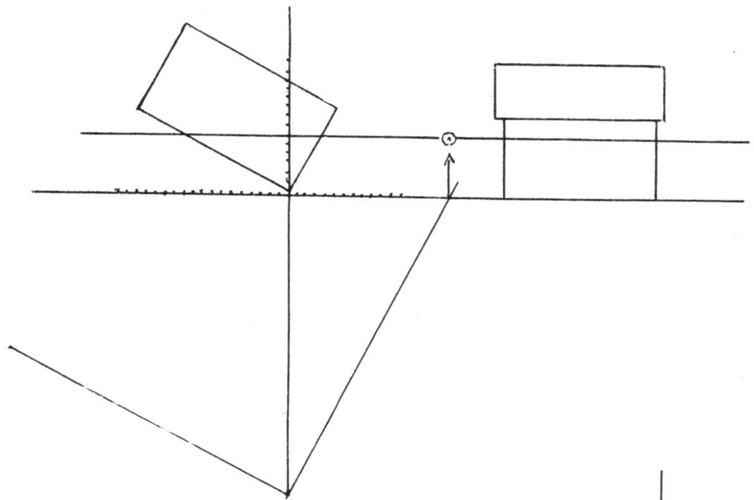

THROUGH ANY POINT ON THE GROUND DRAW A PERPENDICULAR LINE. SCALE OFF FOOT LENGTHS ON THE LINES STARTING FROM THIS POINT.

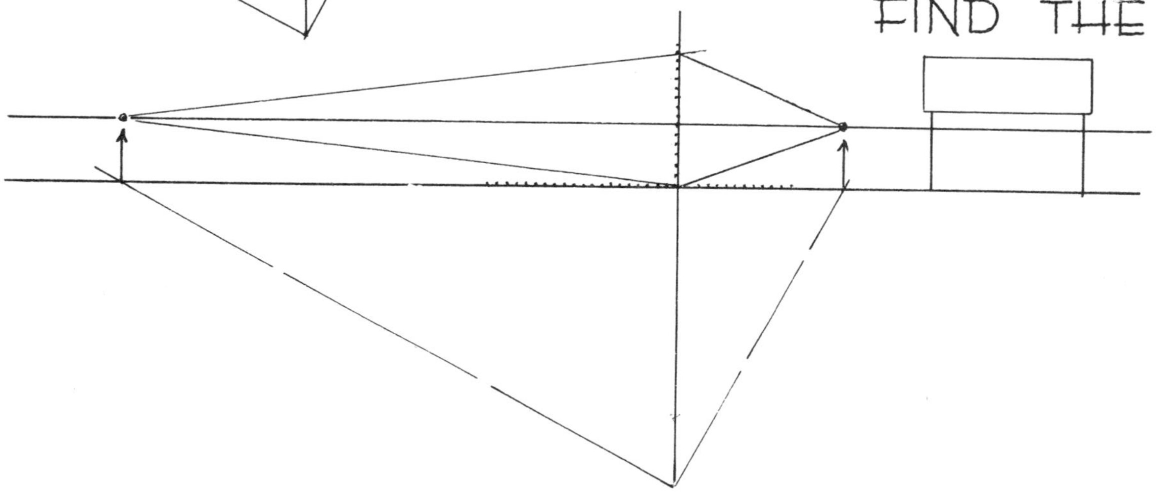

FIND THE HEIGHT ON THE MEASURING LINE AND EXTEND TO THE VANISHING POINTS ON THE HORIZON.

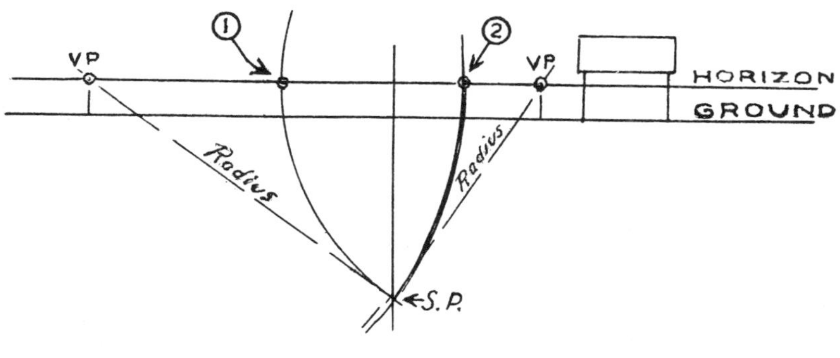

WITH A COMPASS USE THE TWO VANISHING POINTS AS CIRCLE CENTERS AND DRAW ARCS FROM S.P. TO THE HORIZON.

FINISH BY MEASURING THE HOUSE (8 FT. x 16 FT.) AND DRAWING LINES FROM ① AND ② TO WHERE THOSE MEASUREMENTS COME ON THE GROUND LINE. DRAW UPRIGHT LINES WHERE THEY CROSS D AND E.

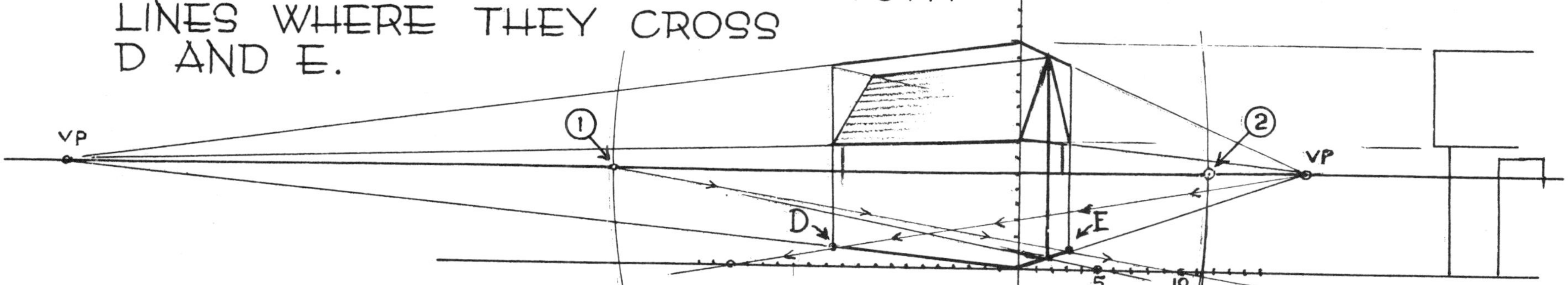

THREE KINDS OF PERSPECTIVE

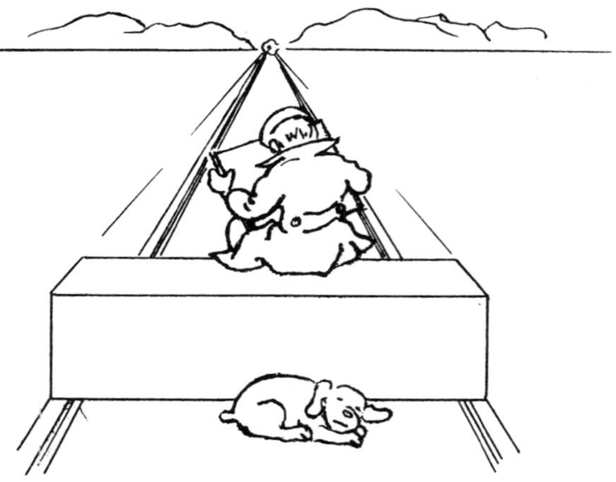

ONE POINT PERSPECTIVE IS DRAWN AS IF WE WERE DRAWING A RAILROAD TRACK.

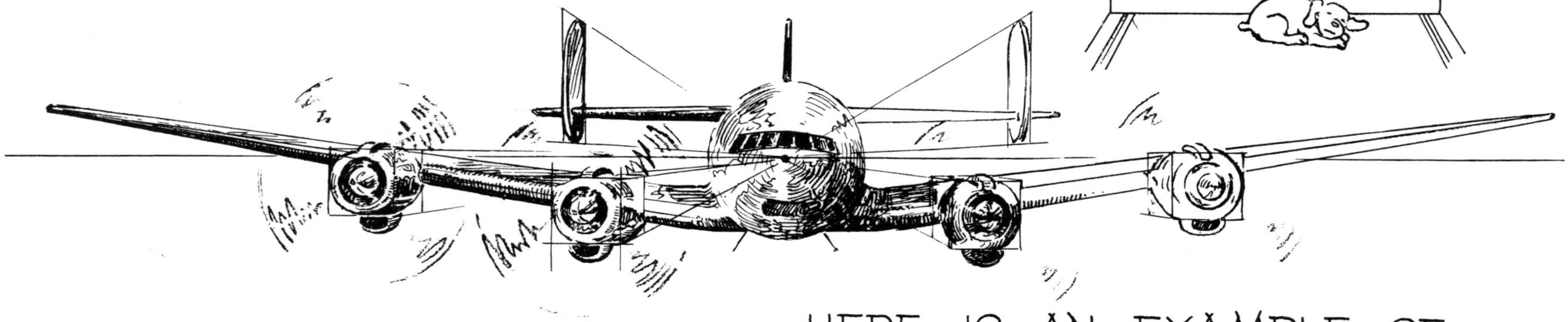

HERE IS AN EXAMPLE OF ONE POINT PERSPECTIVE

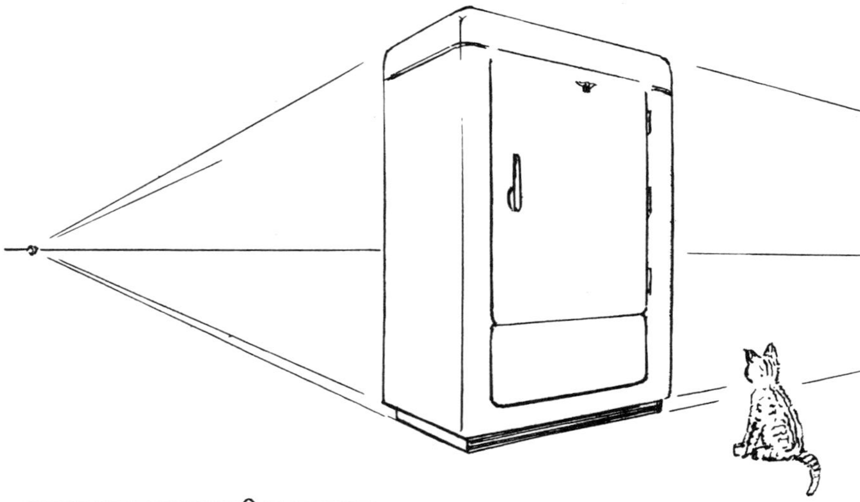

WE ARE FAMILIAR WITH TWO POINT PERSPECTIVE.

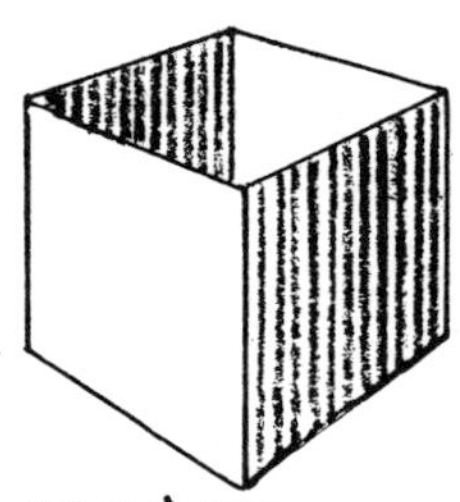

2 POINT

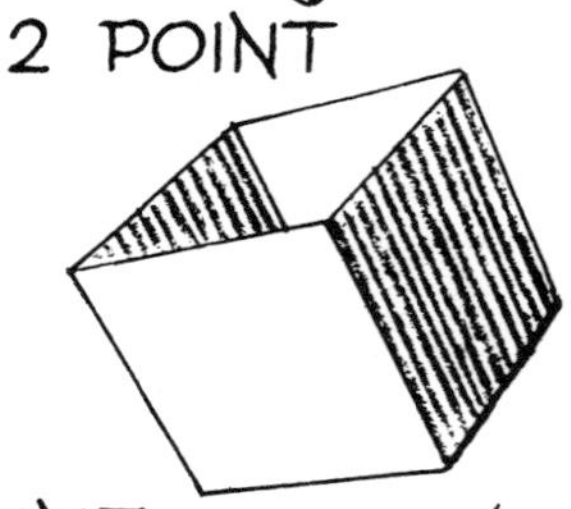

3 POINT

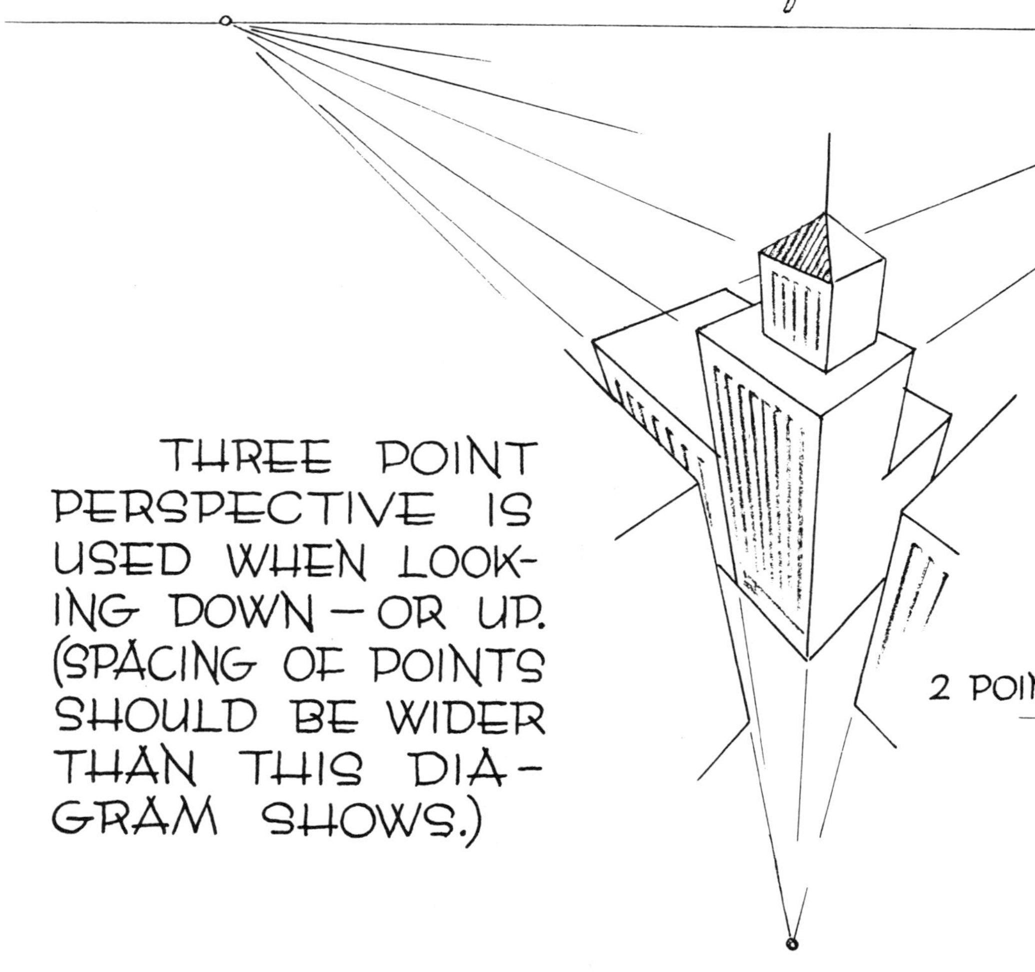

THREE POINT PERSPECTIVE IS USED WHEN LOOKING DOWN—OR UP. (SPACING OF POINTS SHOULD BE WIDER THAN THIS DIAGRAM SHOWS.)

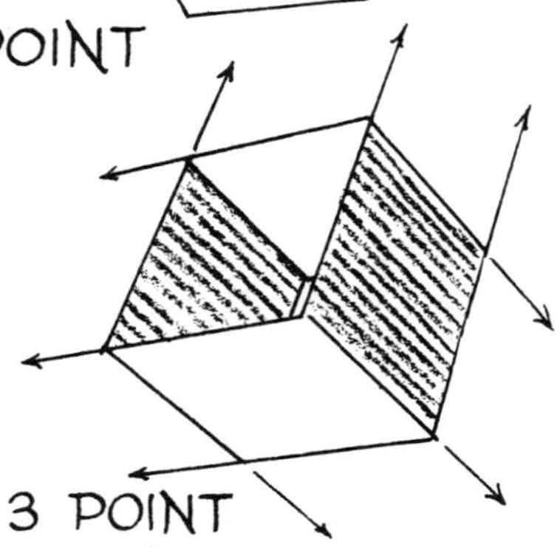

3 POINT

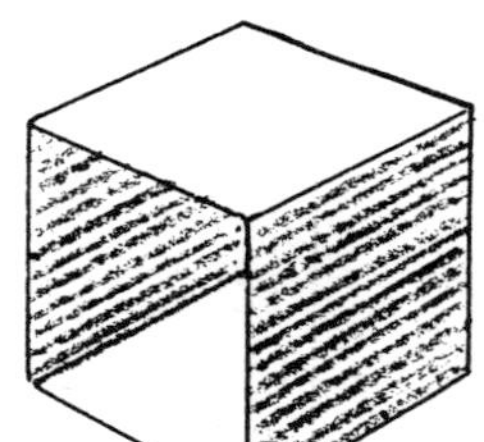

2 POINT

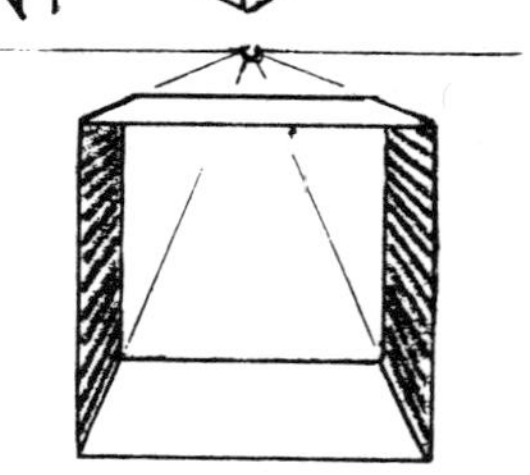

1 POINT

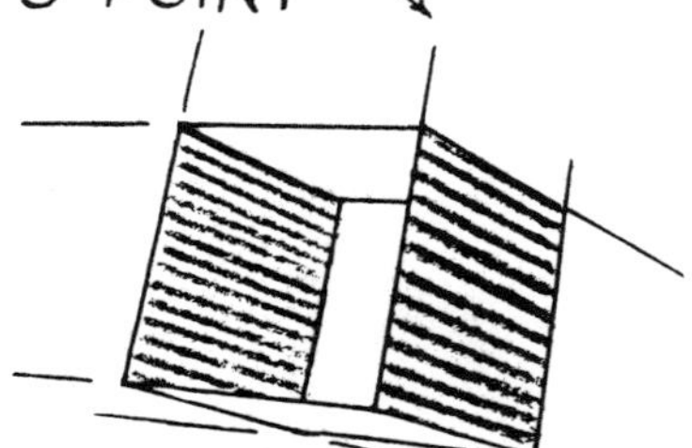

3 POINT

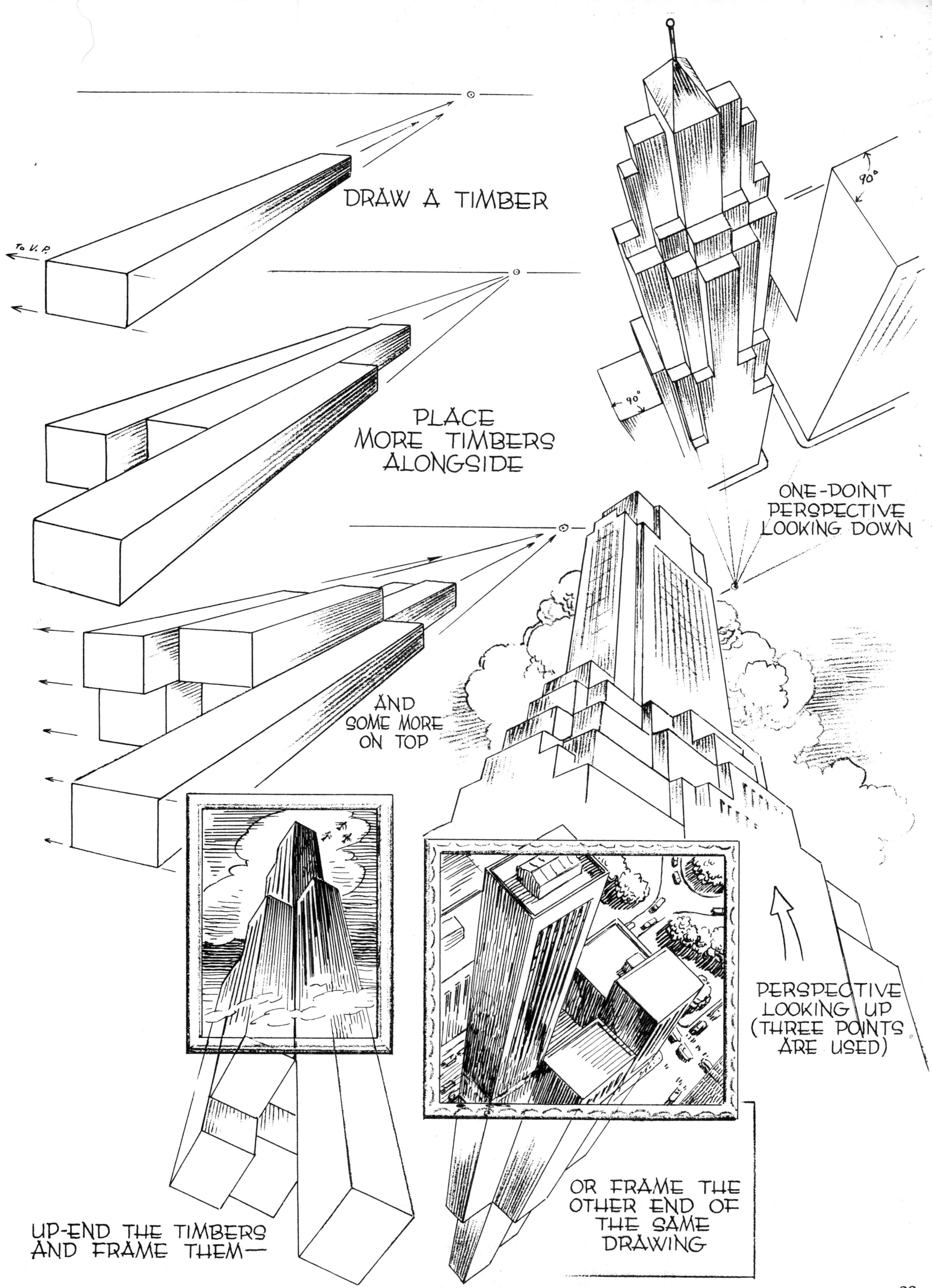
DRAW A TIMBER
TO V. P.
PLACE MORE TIMBERS ALONGSIDE
AND SOME MORE ON TOP
90°
90°
ONE-POINT PERSPECTIVE LOOKING DOWN
PERSPECTIVE LOOKING UP (THREE POINTS ARE USED)
UP-END THE TIMBERS AND FRAME THEM—
OR FRAME THE OTHER END OF THE SAME DRAWING

THE CIRCLE IN PERSPECTIVE IS AN ELLIPSE

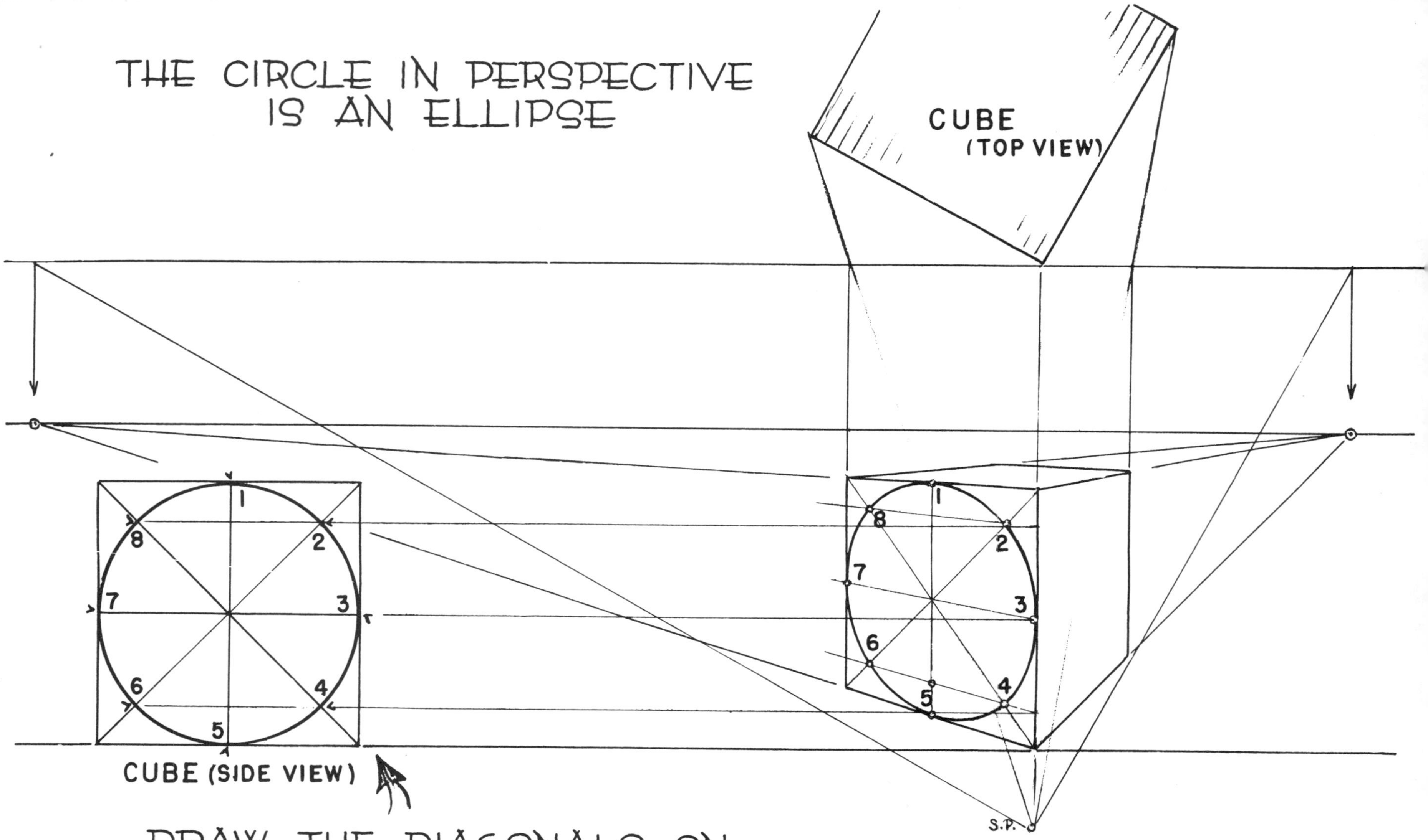

DRAW THE DIAGONALS ON THE SIDE VIEW. THEY CROSS AT THE CENTER OF THE CIRCLE. DRAW THE CIRCLE.

CIRCLES IN A SQUARE TOUCH AT 4 POINTS

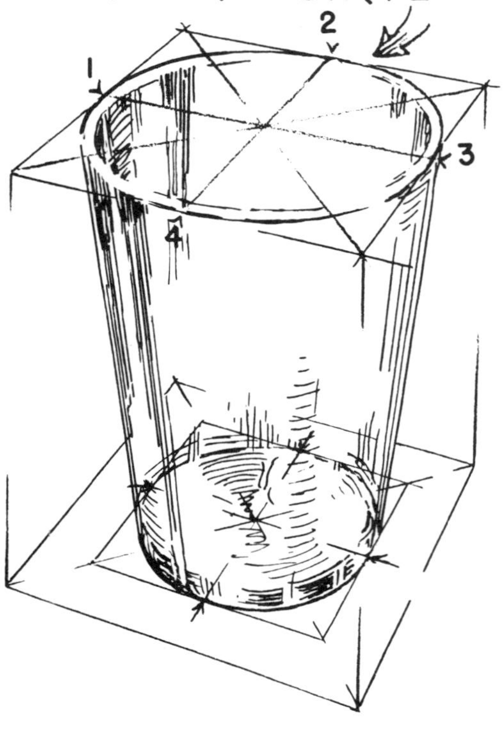

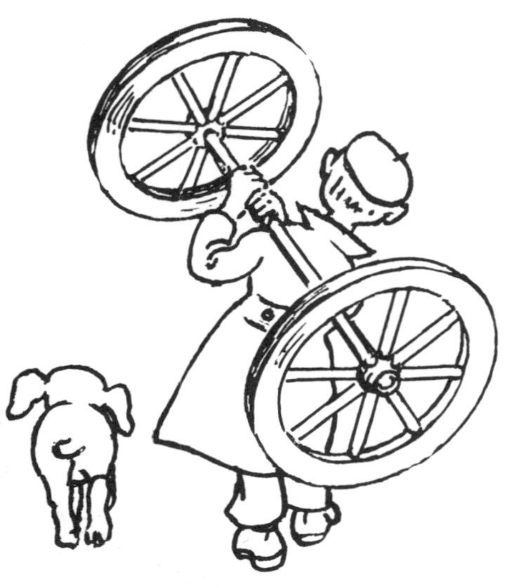

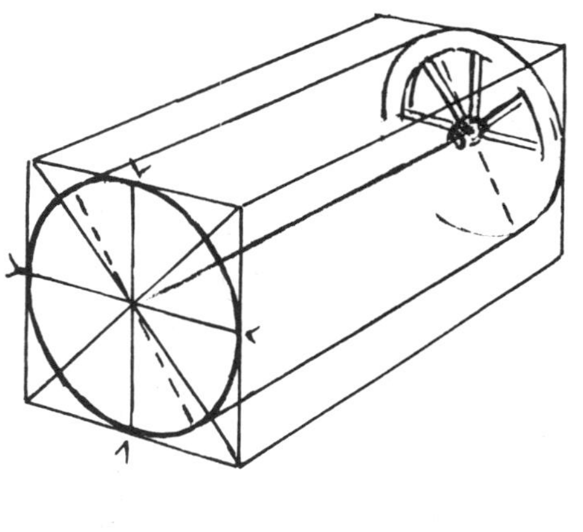

A CYLINDER IS LIKE A PAIR OF WHEELS ON AN AXEL. ALWAYS DRAW THE LONG LINE OF THE ELLIPSE — (CALLED THE MAJOR AXIS) — SO IT MAKES A RIGHT ANGLE WITH THE AXLE.

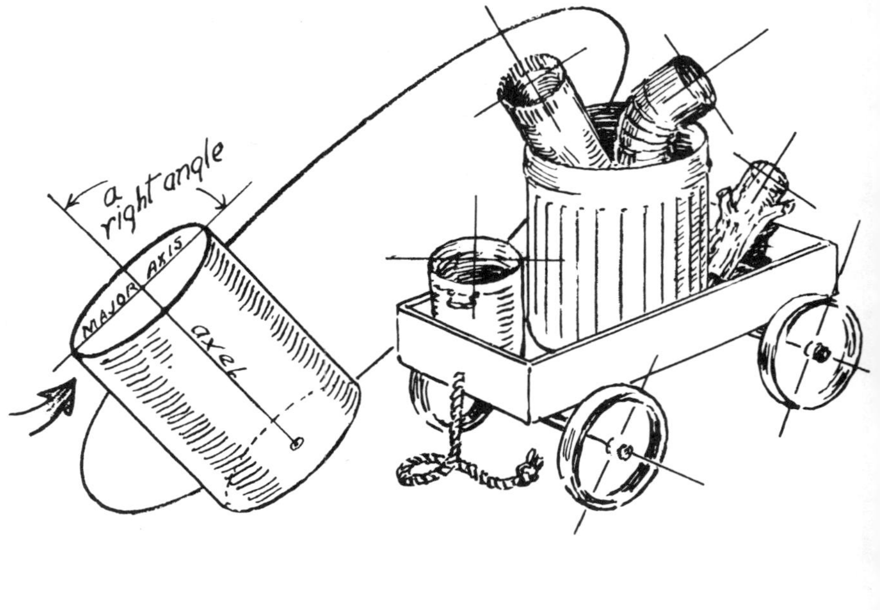

DIVIDING A CIRCLE IN PERSPECTIVE

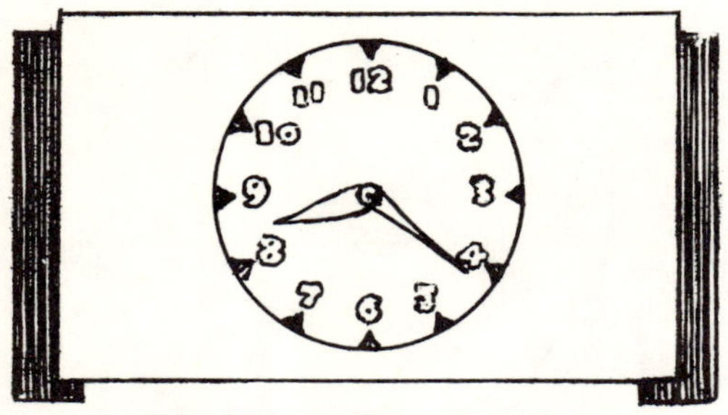

THE CLOCK

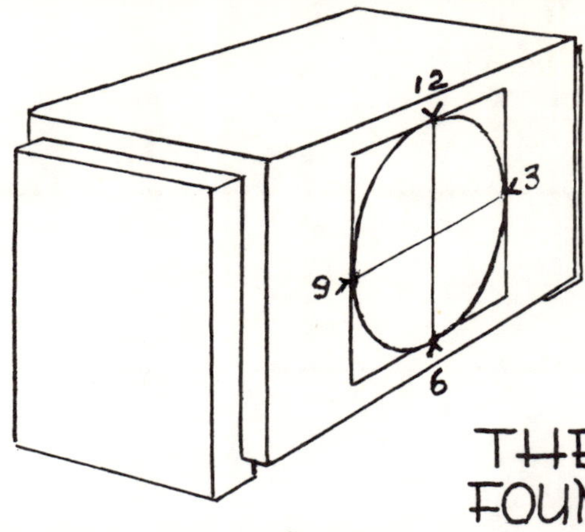

FIRST YOU DRAW THE CLOCK IN PERSPECTIVE. DRAW A SQUARE WHICH REPRESENTS THE DIAL. THE LOCATION OF THE ELLIPSE CAN BE FOUND WHERE IT TOUCHES THE SQUARE AT 12, 3, 6 AND 9 OCLOCK. NOW TO FIND THE LOCATION OF THE HOURS.

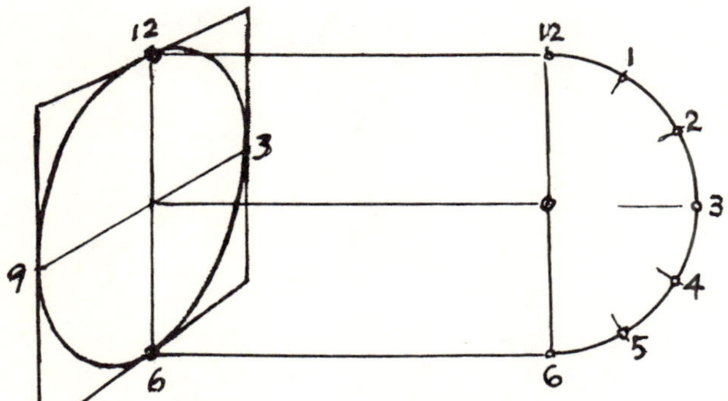

FIRST——

DRAW LINES STRAIGHT OUT FROM THE CENTER OF THE CLOCK AND FROM "12" AND "6"

THEN FILL THE SPACE WITH A COMPASS CIRCLE AND LOCATE THE HOURS "12" TO "6".

SOME SHORTCUTS

THIS GEAR HAS TWELVE COGS LET US SKETCH THEM IN!

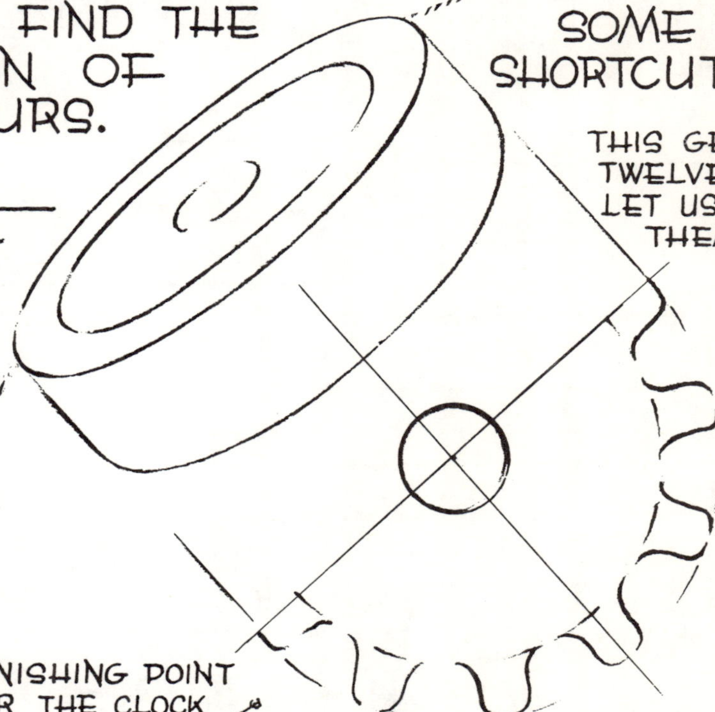

VANISHING POINT FOR THE CLOCK

SO FIRST YOU DRAW HALF THE GEAR WITH A COMPASS SHOWING THE COGS.

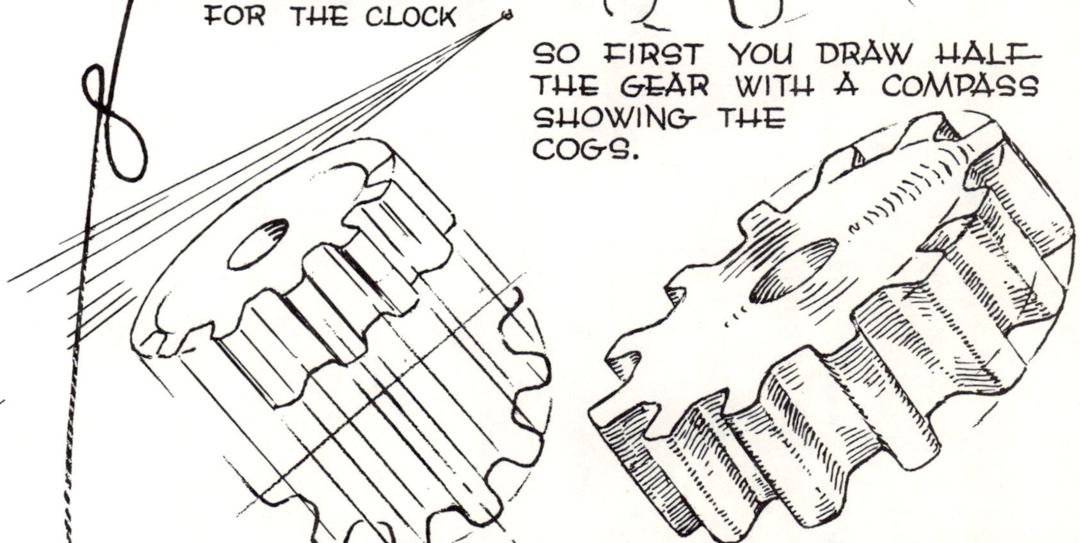

NOW YOU DRAW LINES AS SHOWN FROM THE PLAN TO THE CORRESPONDING POINTS ON THE WHEEL.

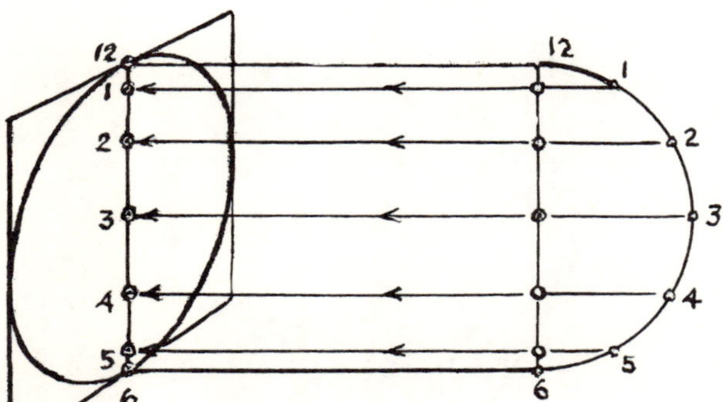

FROM HERE WE MAKE LINES TO FIND NEW POINTS.

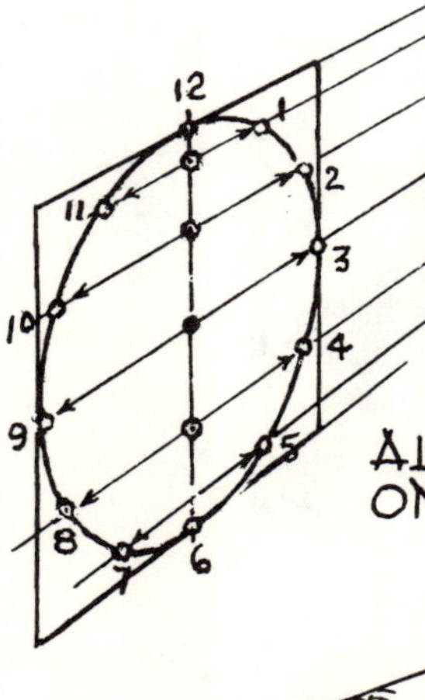

LINES DRAWN THROUGH THESE POINTS TO THE VANISHING POINT LOCATE ALL THE NUMBERS ON THE DIAL.

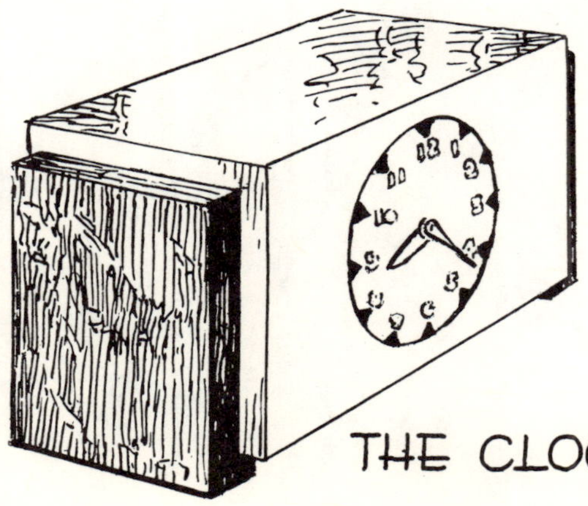

THE CLOCK

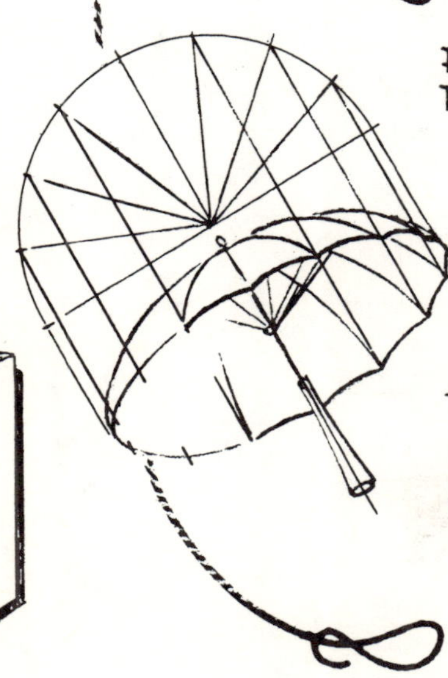

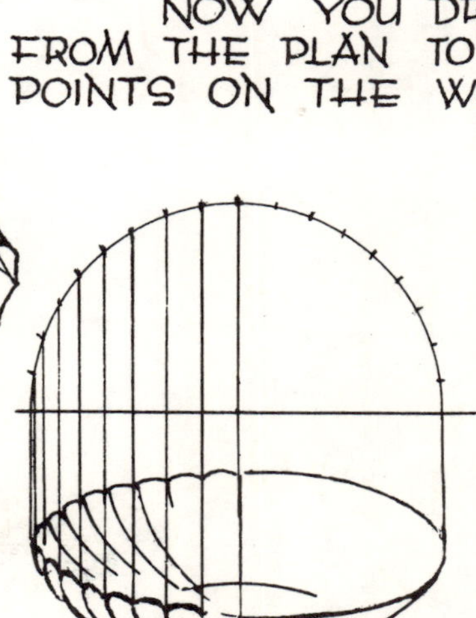

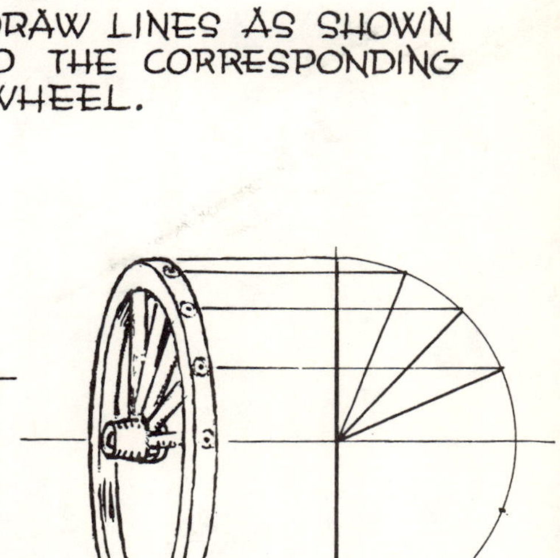

HERE ARE SOME MORE SAMPLES

PERSPECTIVE SPACING

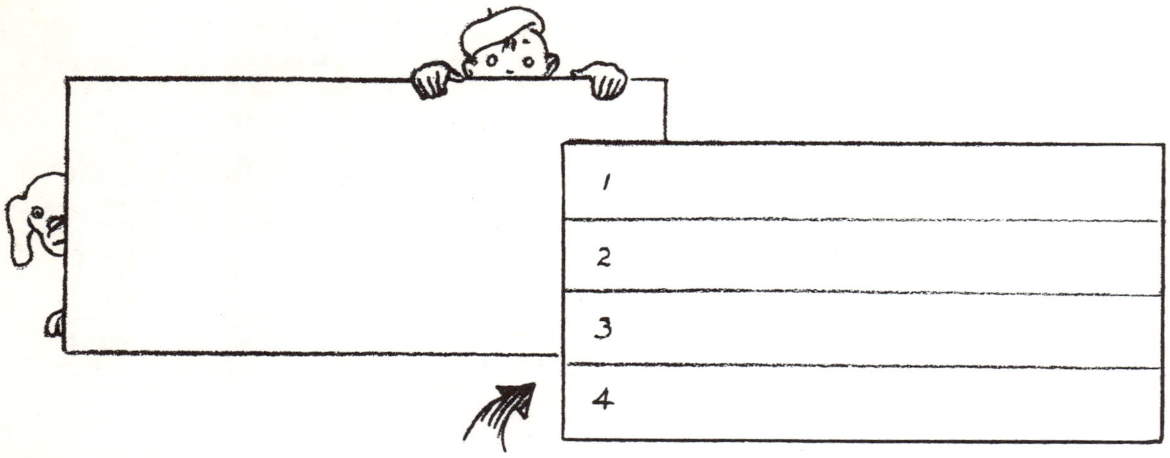

THE SIDE OF A BOX CAN BE DIVIDED INTO EQUAL HORIZONTAL PARTS.

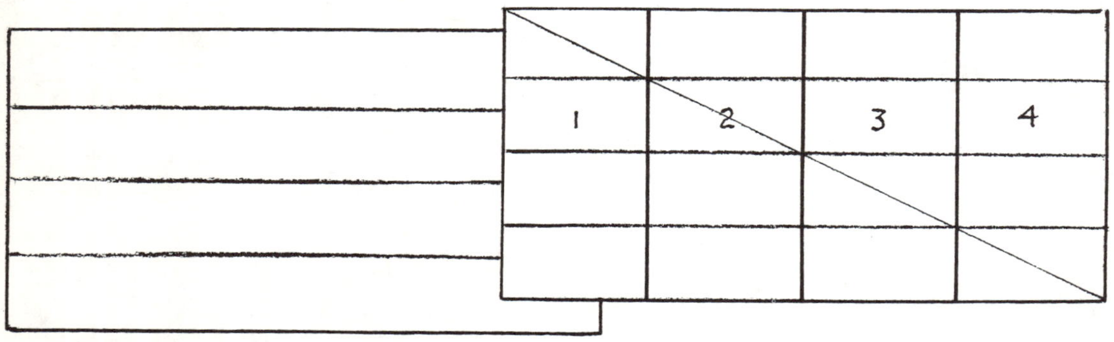

DRAW A DIAGONAL AND NOTE WHERE IT CROSSES THE HORIZONTAL LINES. LINES DRAWN UPRIGHT THROUGH THESE POINTS WILL DIVIDE THE AREA INTO THE SAME NUMBER OF UPRIGHT PARTS.

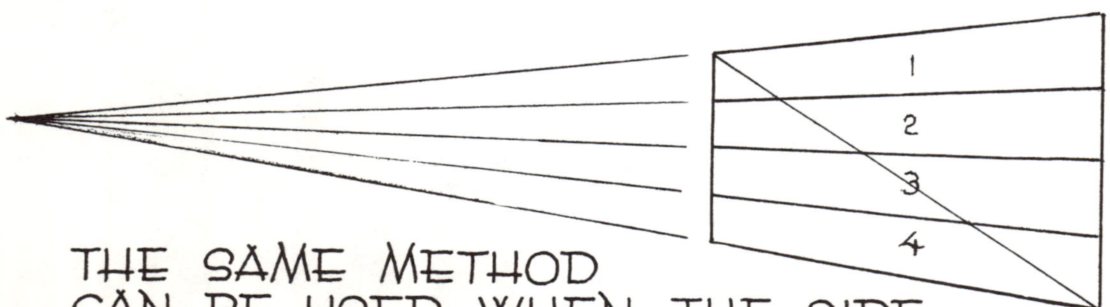

THE SAME METHOD CAN BE USED WHEN THE SIDE OF THE BOX IS DRAWN IN PERSPECTIVE. THE UPRIGHT DIVISIONS ARE IN CORRECT LOCATION AND IN CORRECT PERSPECTIVE.

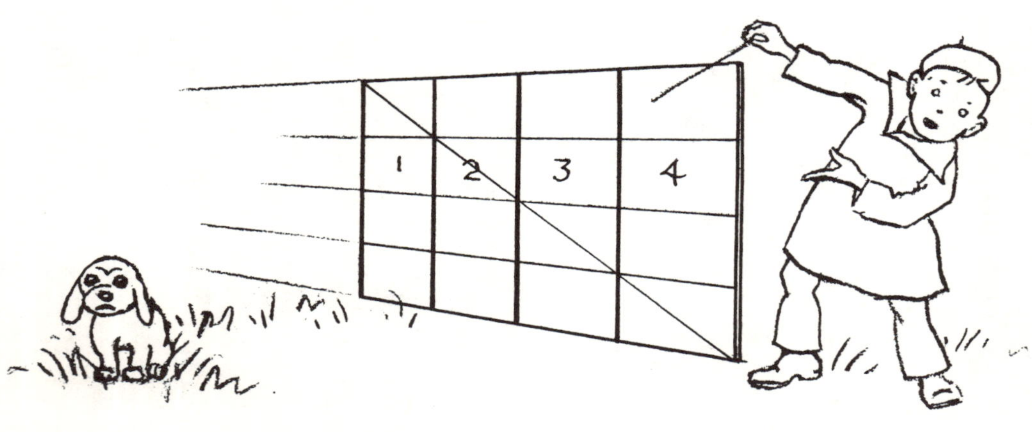

EIGHT BOOKS

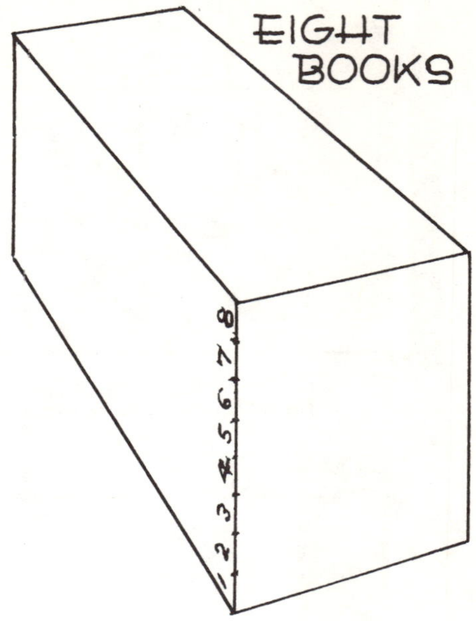

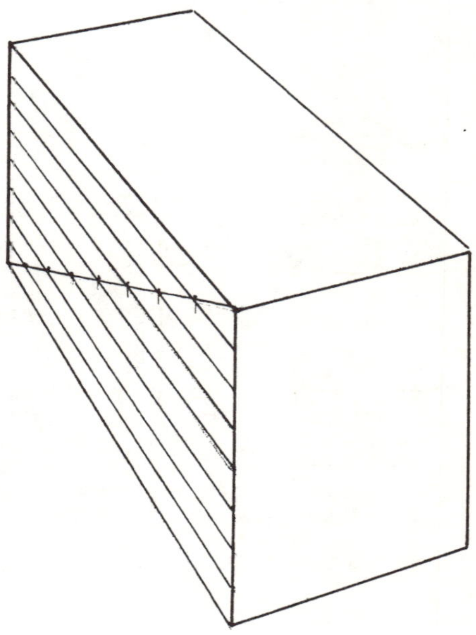

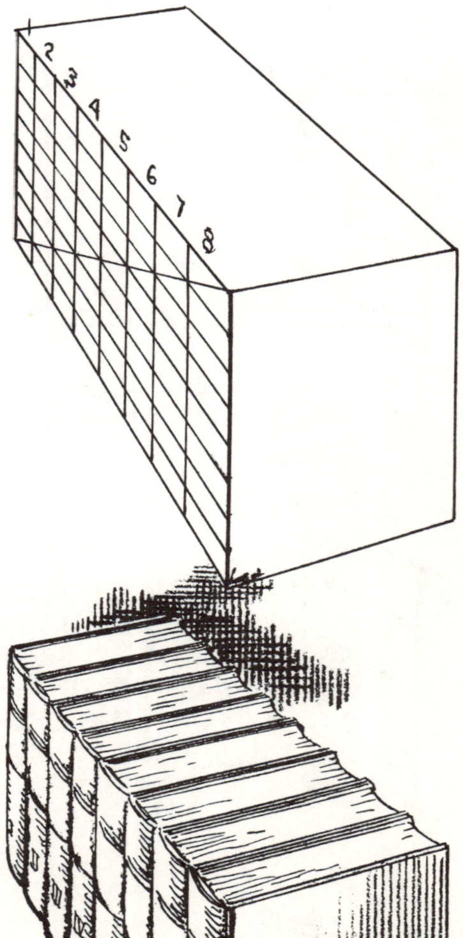

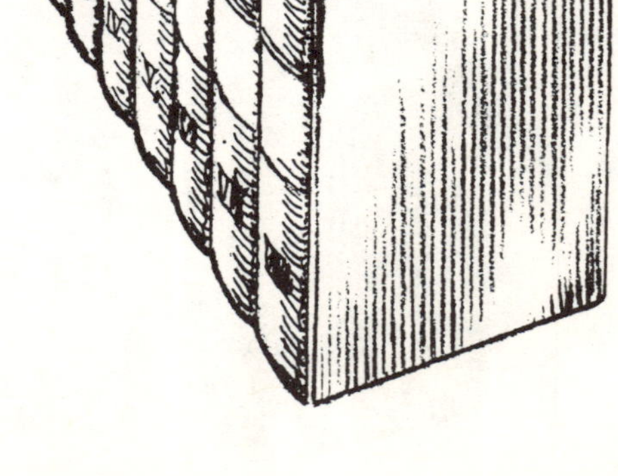

A BIRD HOUSE

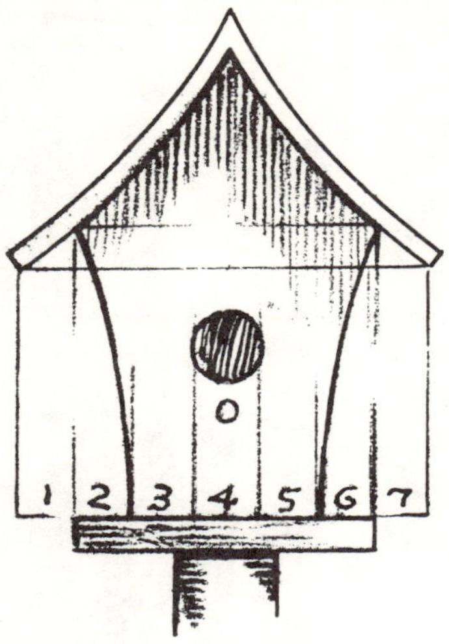

WE NOW KNOW HOW TO DRAW THE FRONT OF A BUILDING— IN PERSPECTIVE.

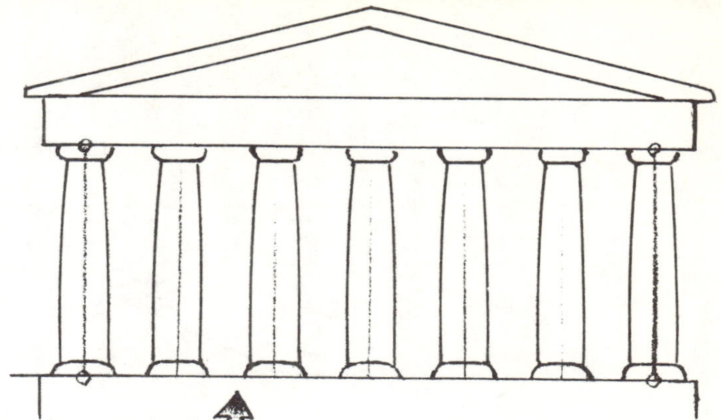

SUCH AS THIS

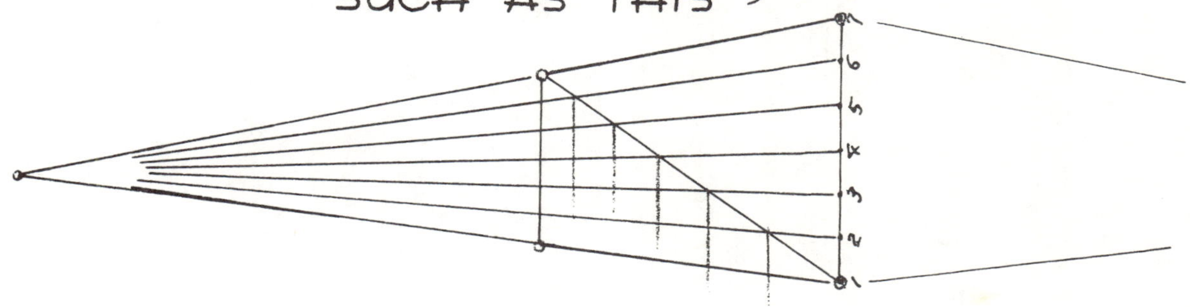

DRAW THE LOWER PART AS IF IT WERE A BOX

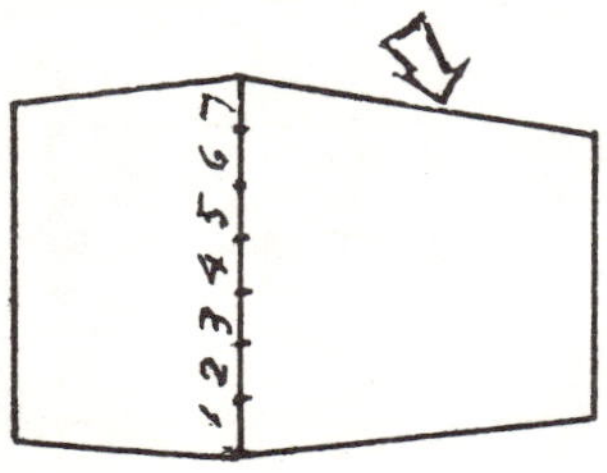

HERE IT IS COMPLETED

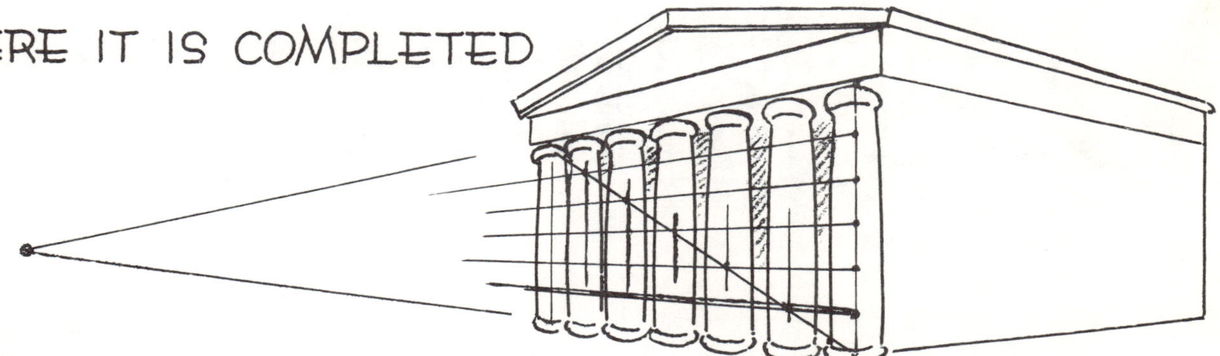

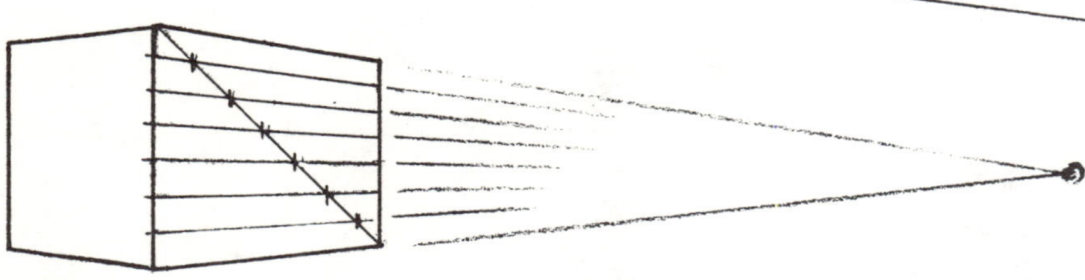

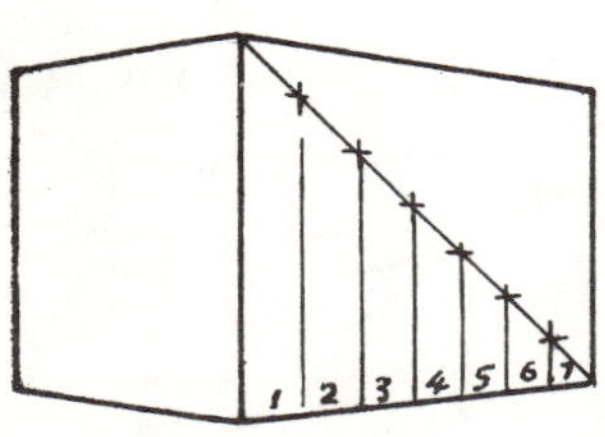

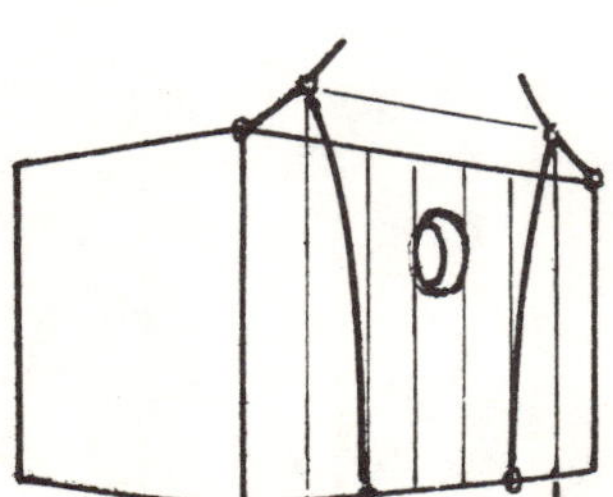

WHEN THE SPACINGS ARE UNEVEN AS SHOWN HERE.

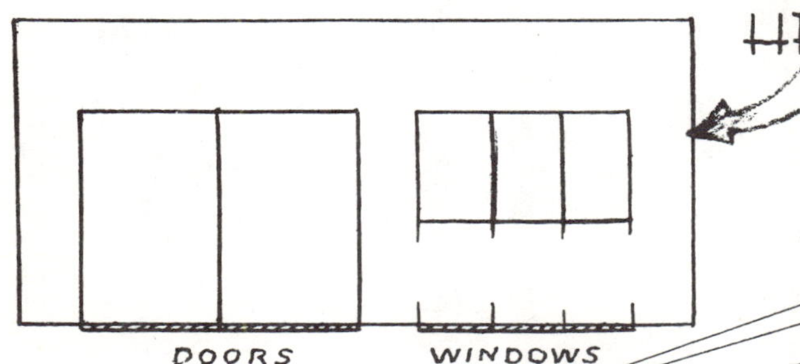

IT WORKS OUT LIKE THIS

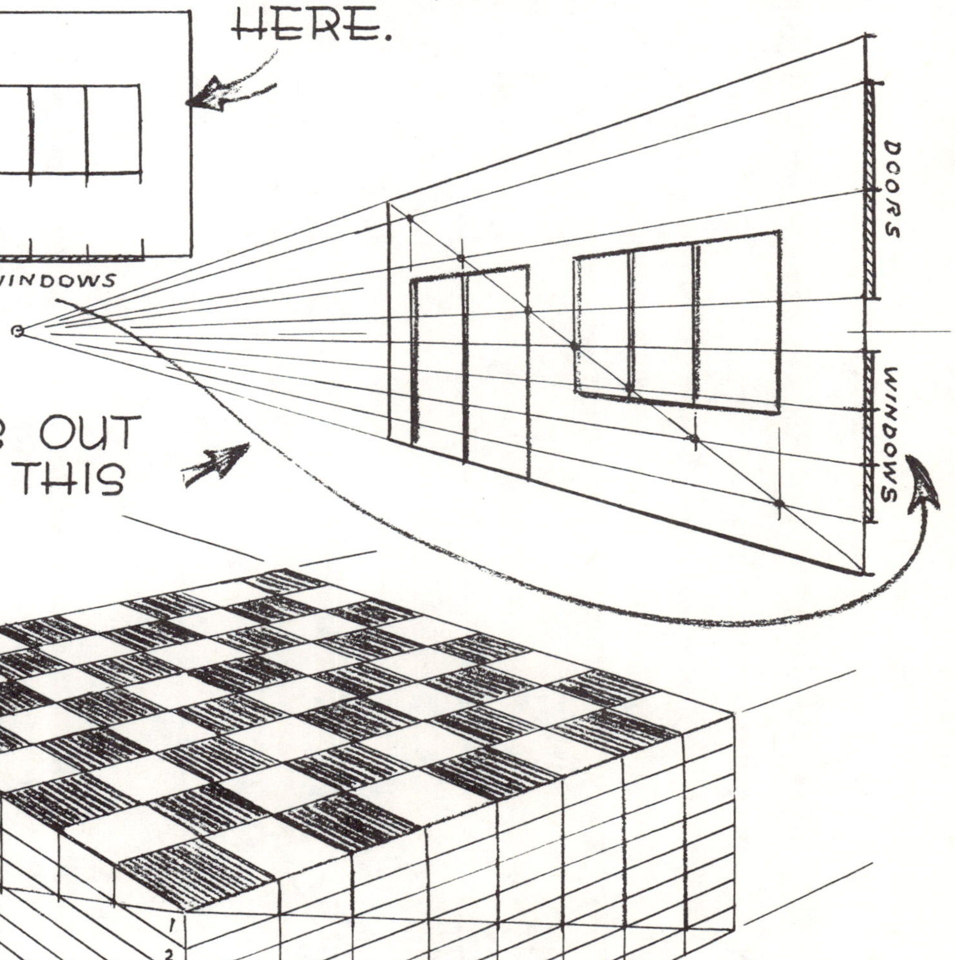

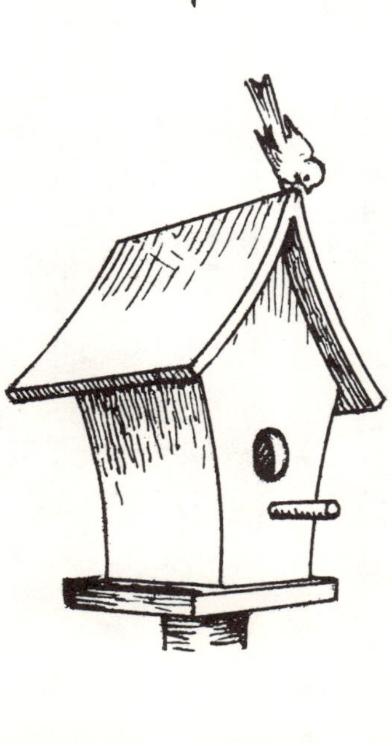

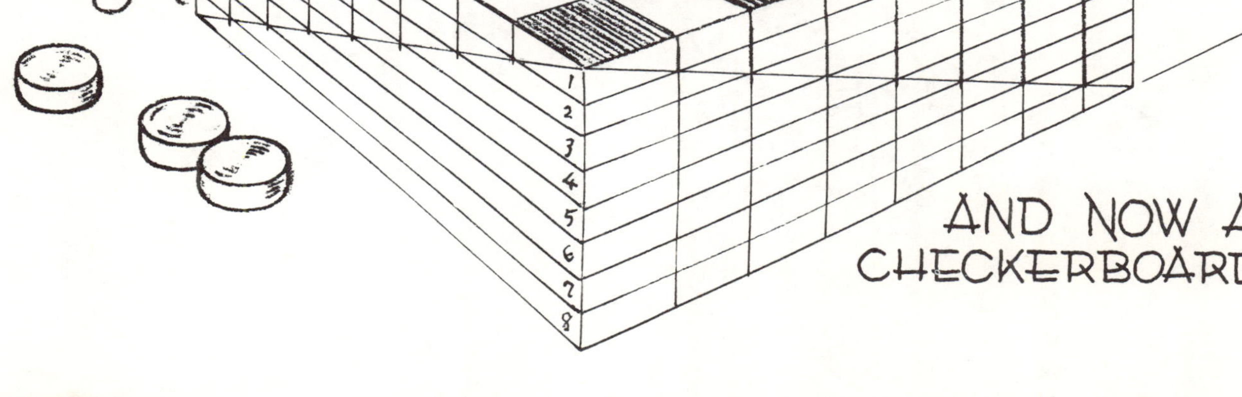

AND NOW A CHECKERBOARD

FIND THE CENTER

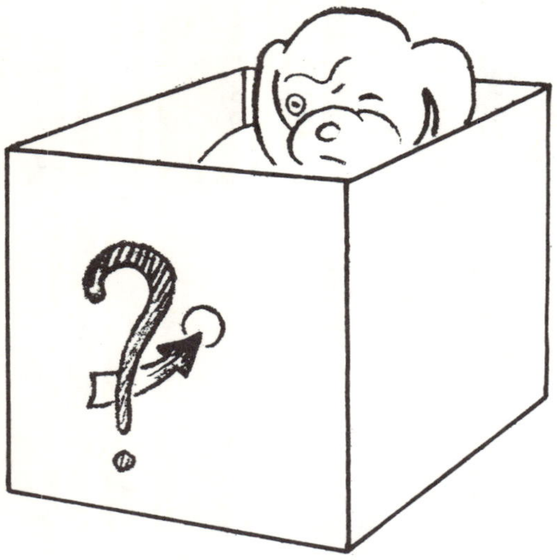

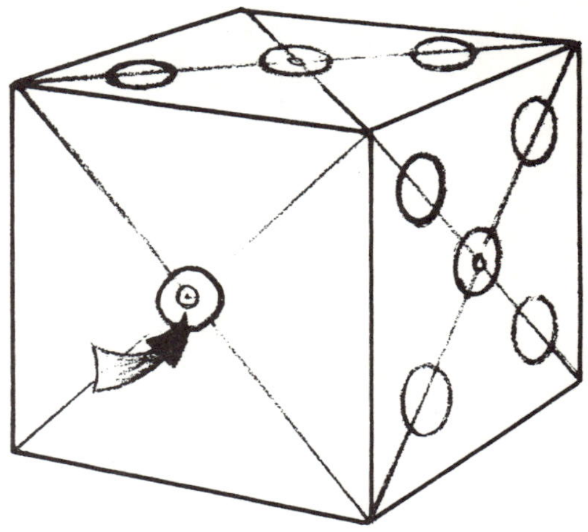

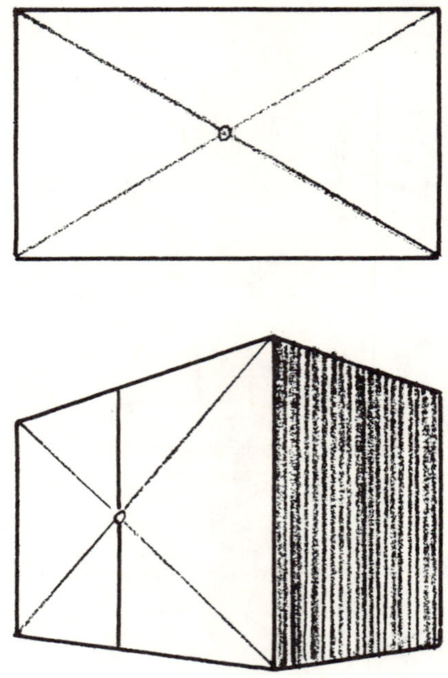

BOX DIVIDED INTO HALVES

TO FIND THE PERSPECTIVE CENTER OF THE SIDES OF THE BOX: DRAW DIAGONAL LINES FROM THE CORNERS. THEY INTERSECT AT THE CENTER.

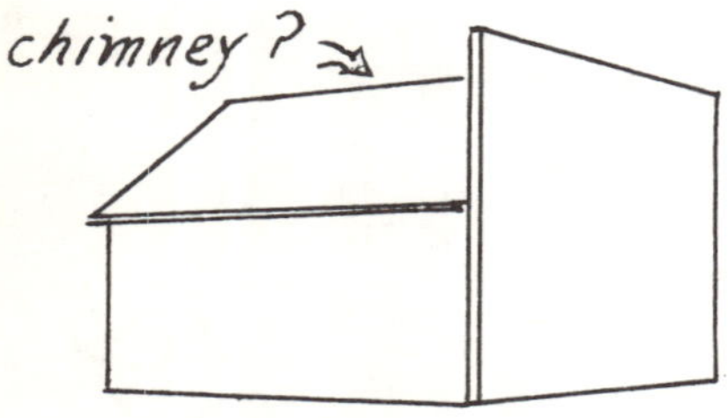

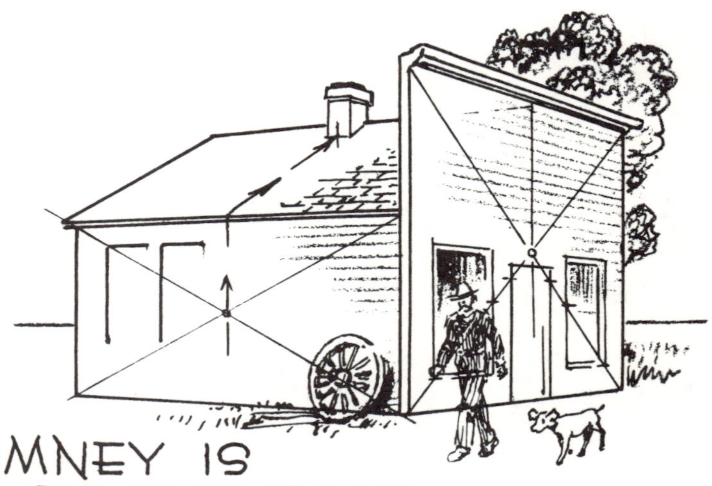

THE DOOR IS IN THE CENTER OF THE BUILDING FRONT. THE CHIMNEY IS IN THE CENTER OF THE ROOF.

HERE ARE MORE CENTERS.

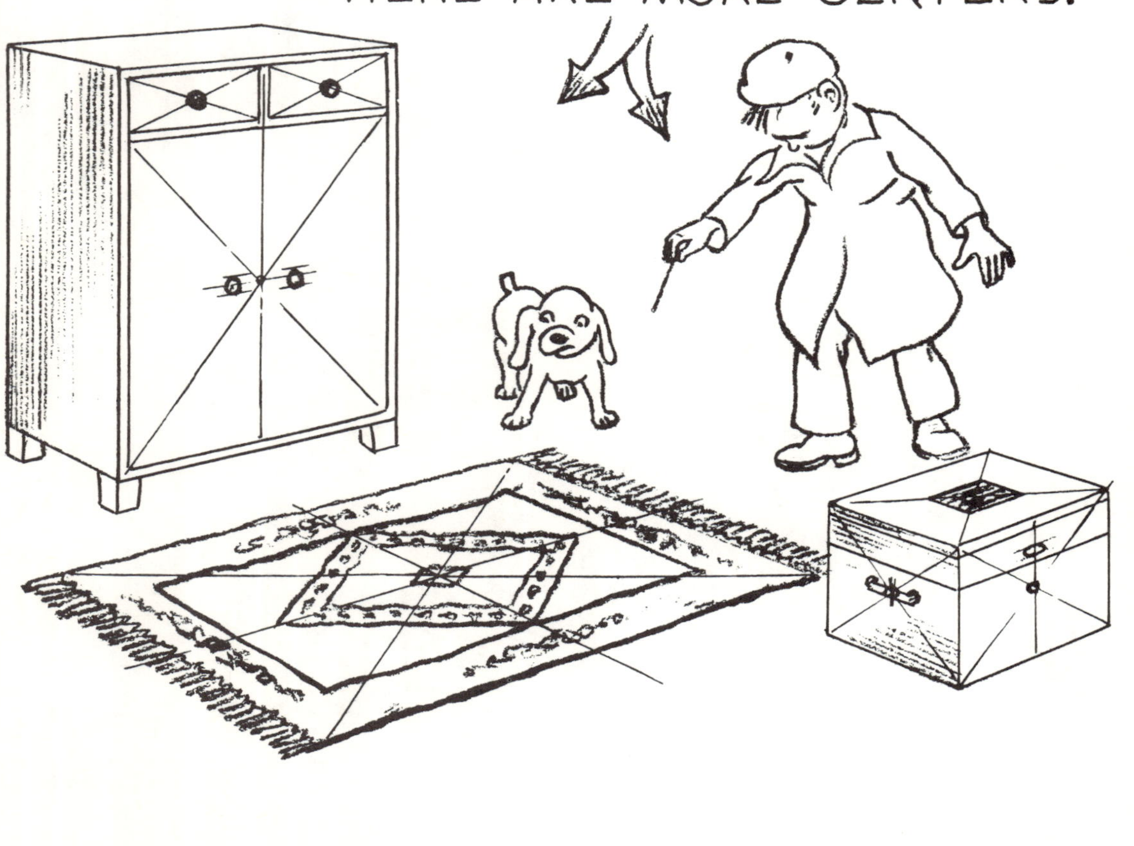

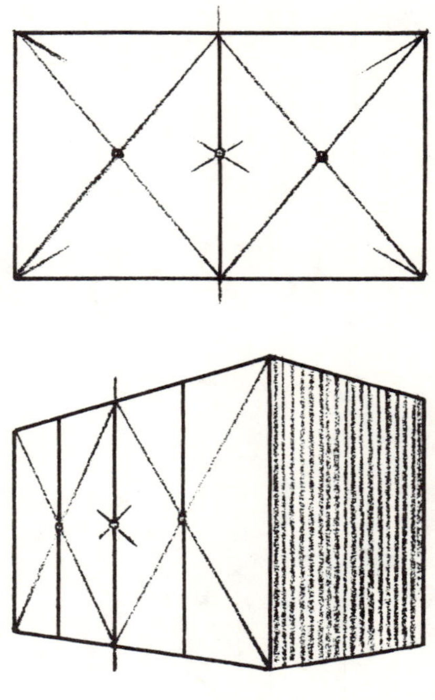

INTO QUARTERS

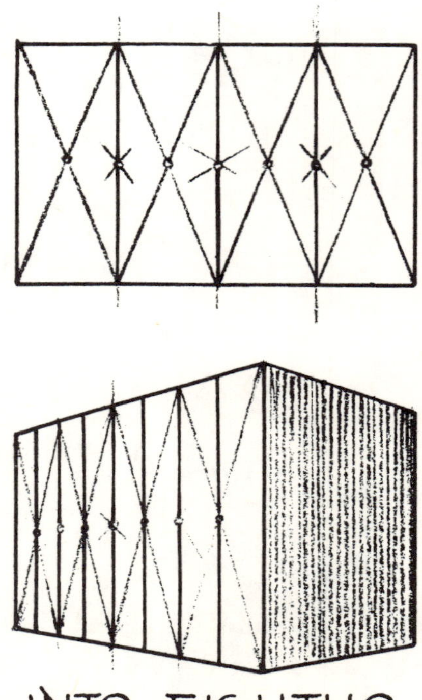

INTO EIGHTHS

EQUAL SPACING IN PERSPECTIVE

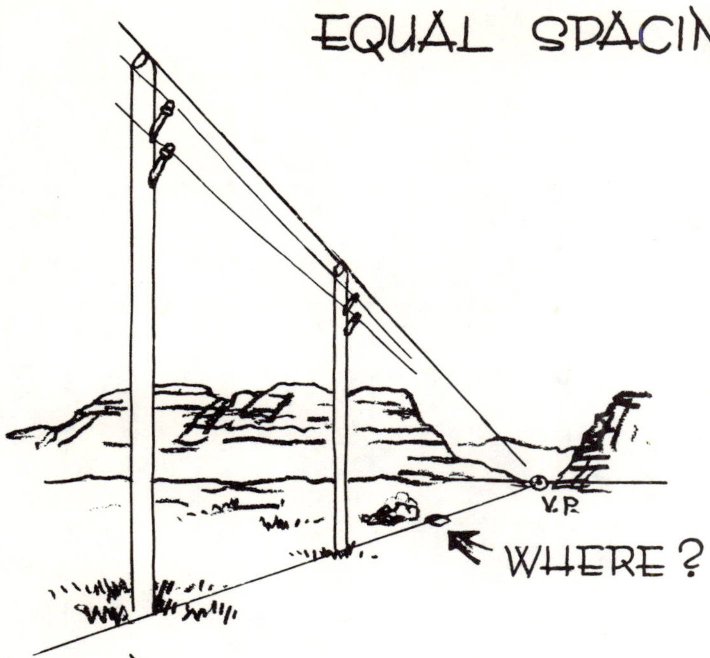

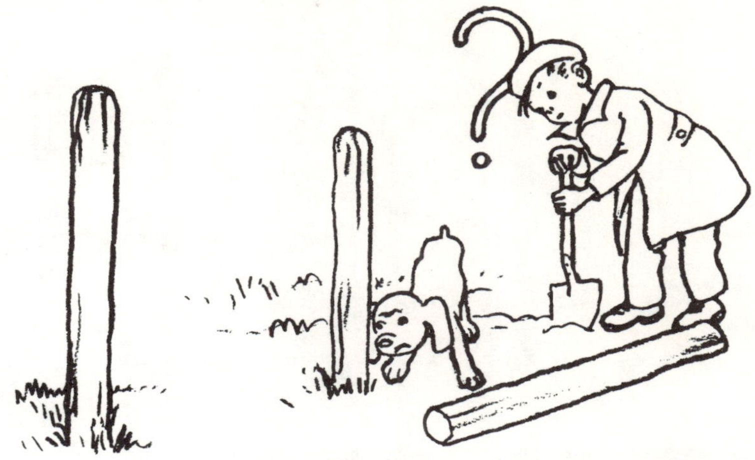

WHERE DOES THE NEXT POST GO?

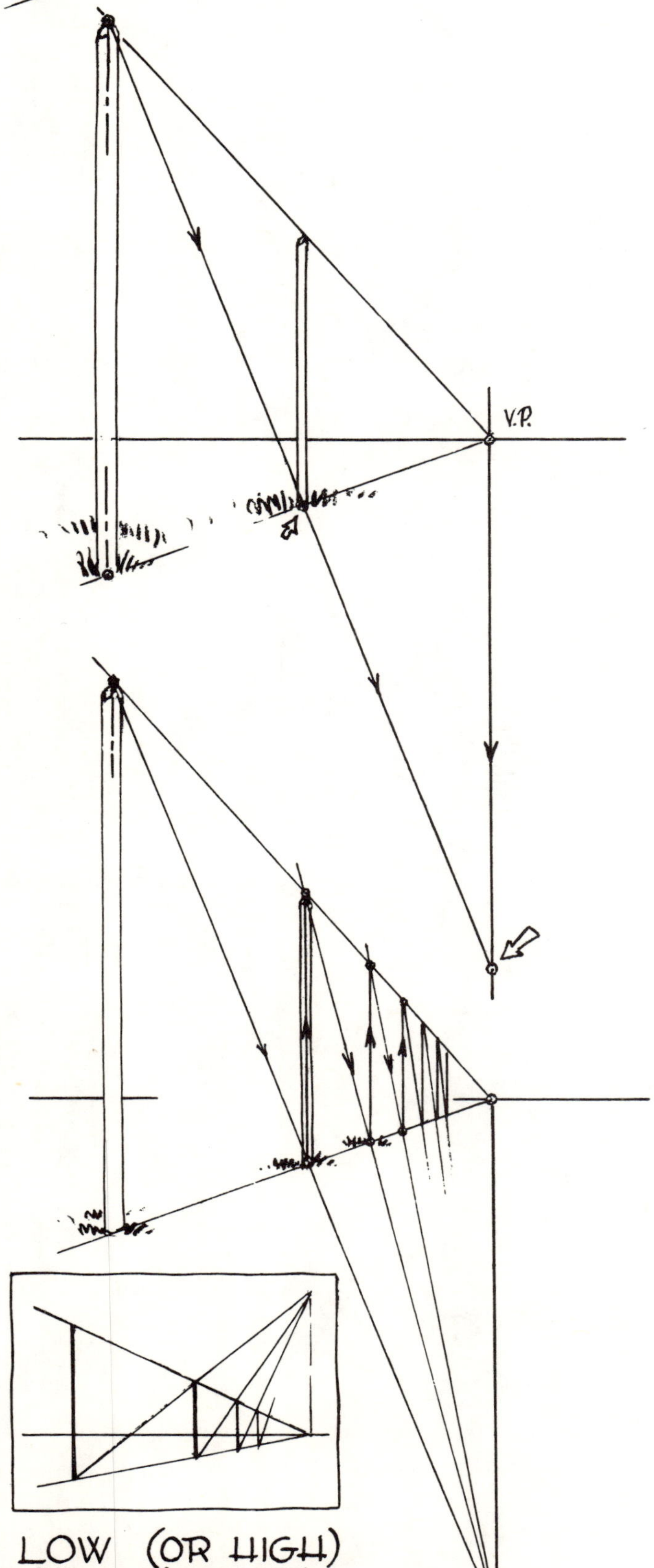

LOW (OR HIGH) VANISHING POINT METHOD

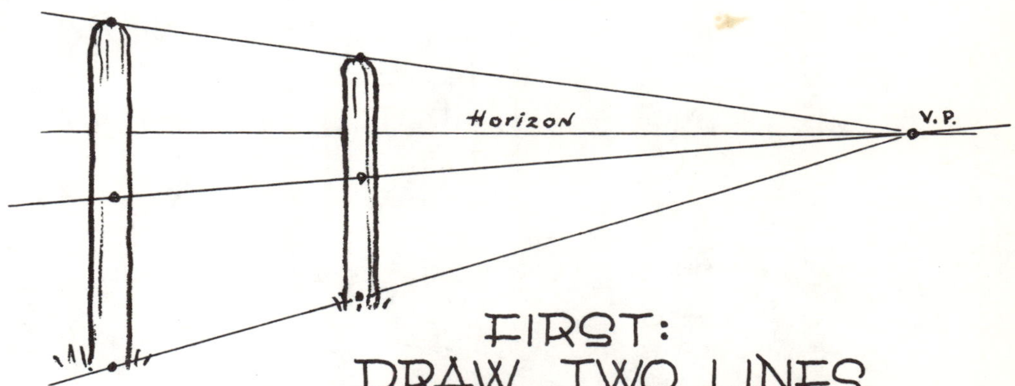

FIRST:
DRAW TWO LINES, ONE ALONG THE TOP OF THE POSTS — THE OTHER ALONG THE BOTTOM. THESE LINES MEET AT THE VANISHING POINT. ANOTHER LINE IS DRAWN HALFWAY BETWEEN.

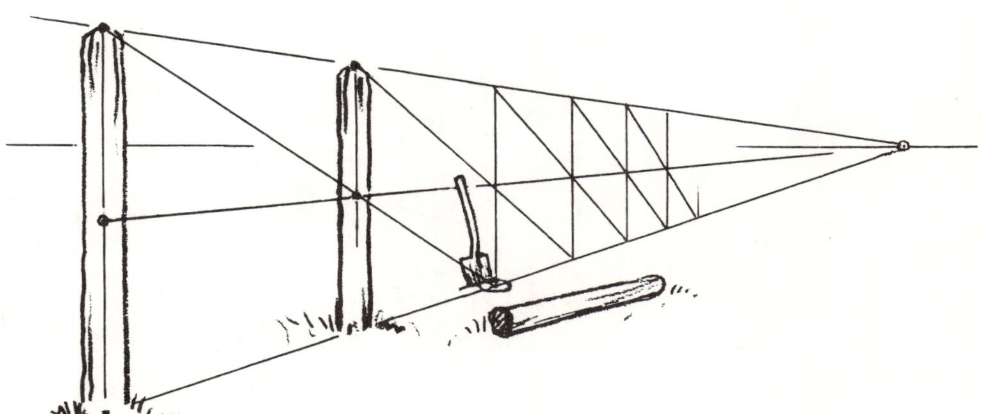

NOW:
DRAW A LINE FROM THE TOP OF THE FIRST POST AND ON THROUGH THE CENTER OF THE SECOND POST TO THE LOWER LINE. WE NOW KNOW WHERE TO PUT THE THIRD POST — AND ALL THE REST.

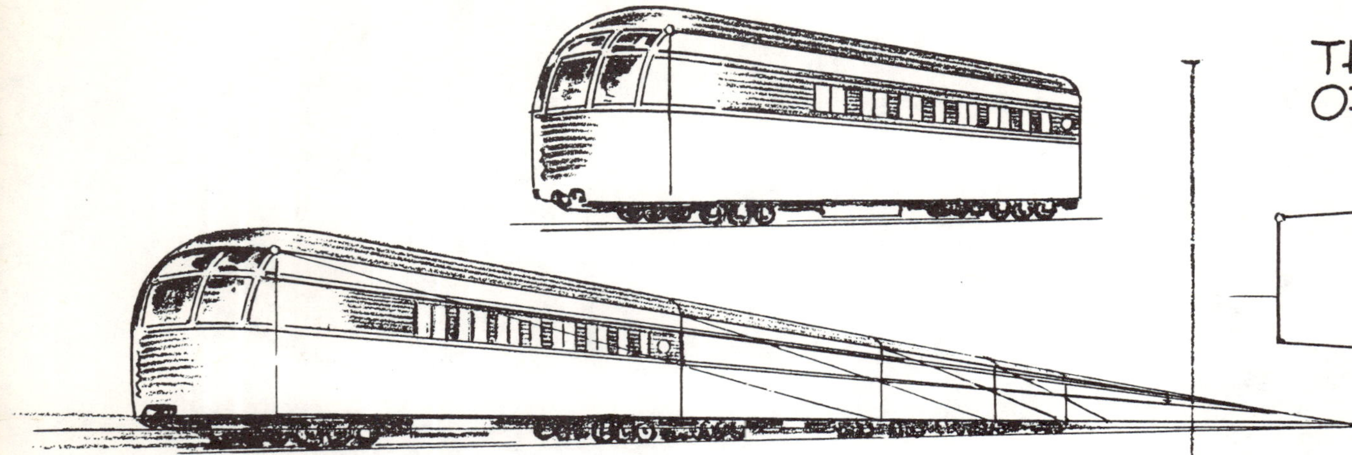

IN THE SAME MANNER YOU CAN MAKE UP A WHOLE TRAIN FROM ONE CAR. FIRST — FIND THE VANISHING POINT — NEXT THE CENTER LINE — THEN THE DIAGONALS.

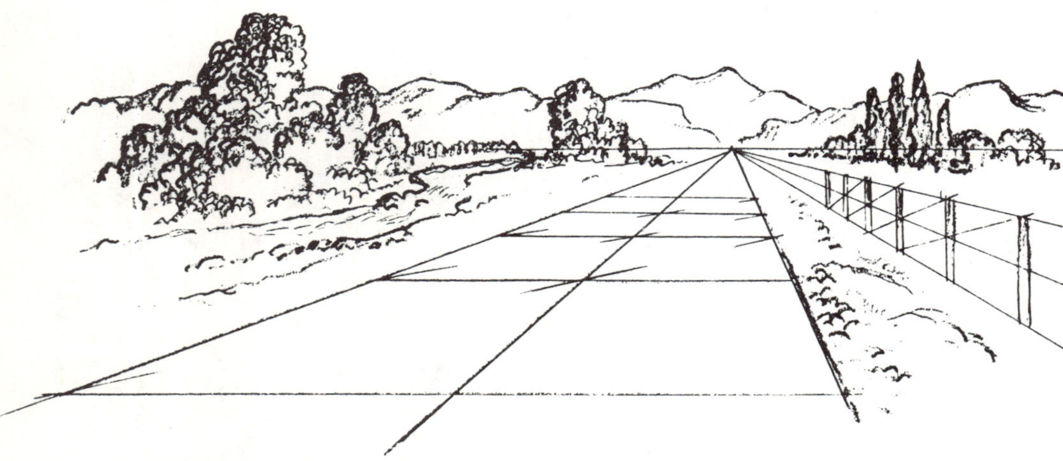

IT WORKS THE SAME ON A FLAT SURFACE SUCH AS THE EXPANSION JOINTS ON A HIGHWAY.

THE SLOPE OF A ROOF.

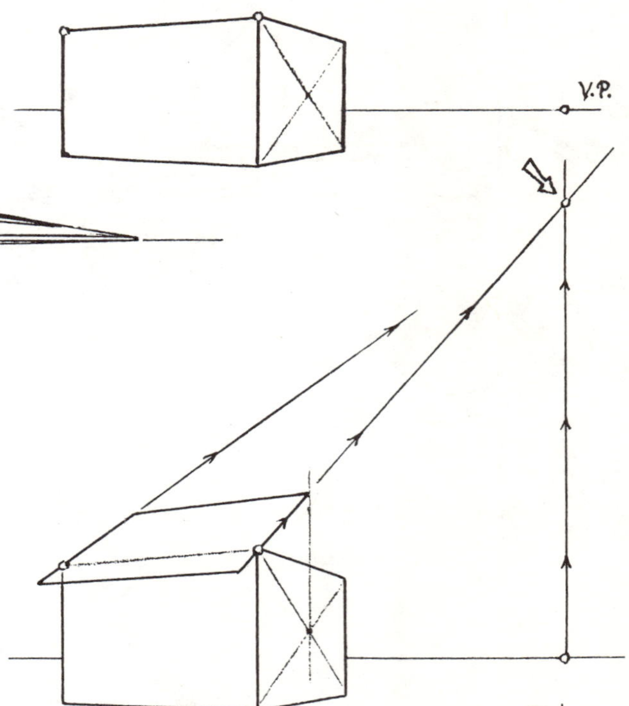

LOWER THE POINT AND FLATTEN THE ROOFS.

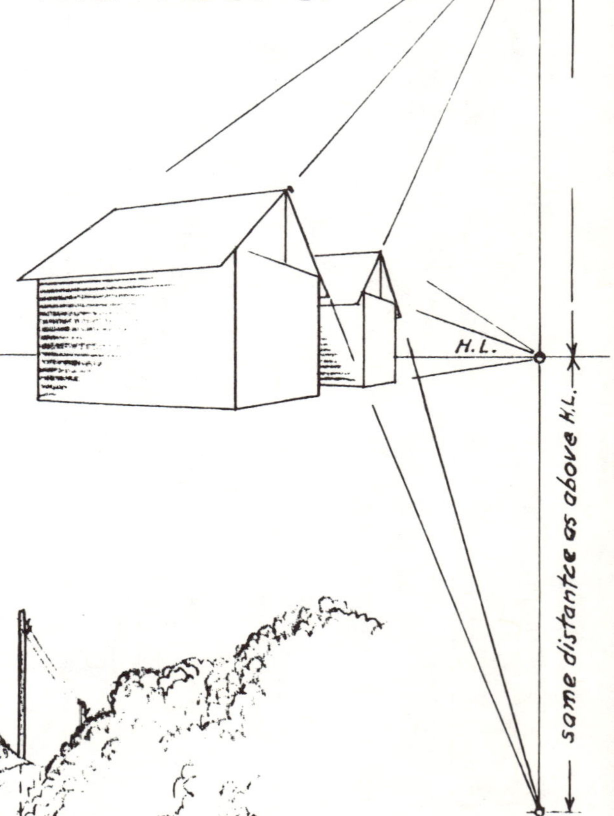

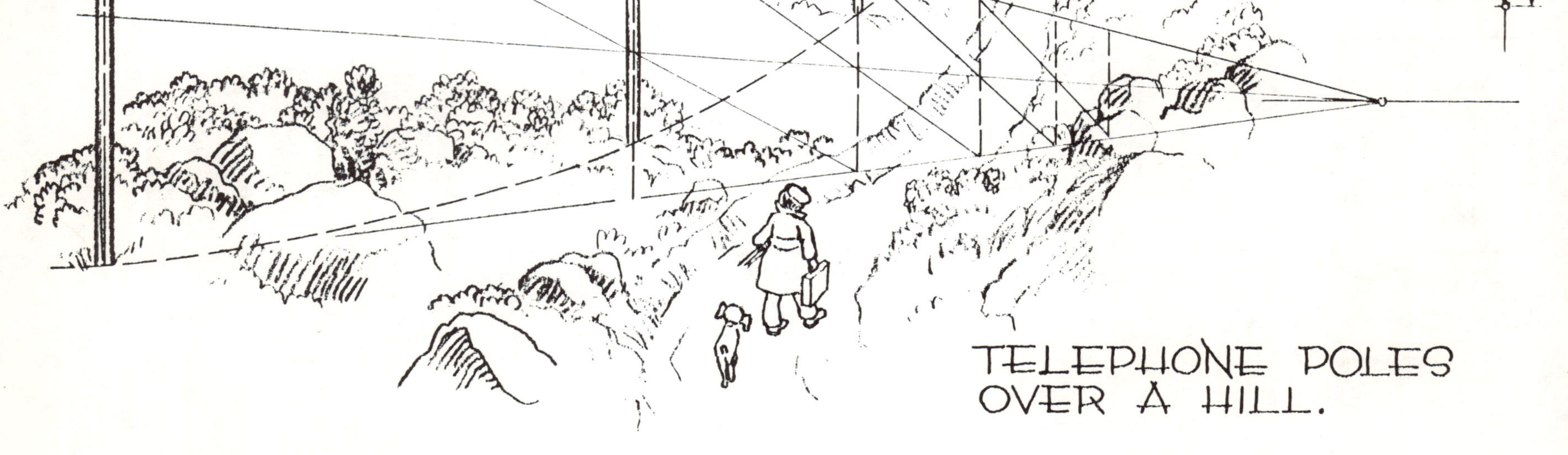

TELEPHONE POLES OVER A HILL.

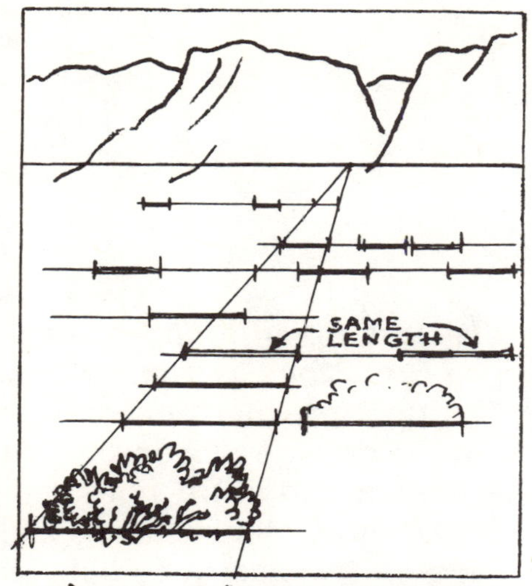

ONE SAGE BRUSH

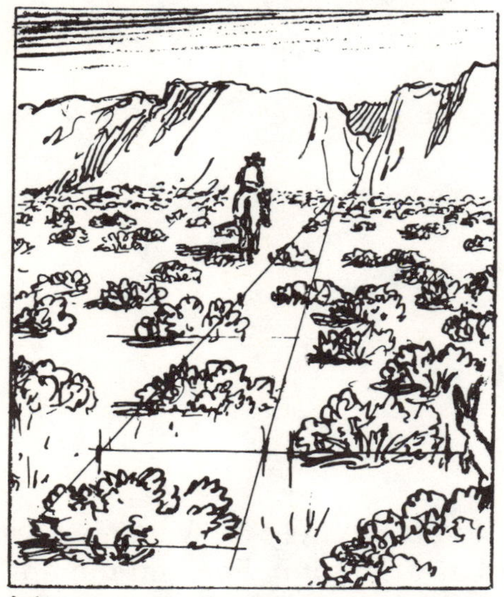

MORE SAGE BRUSHES

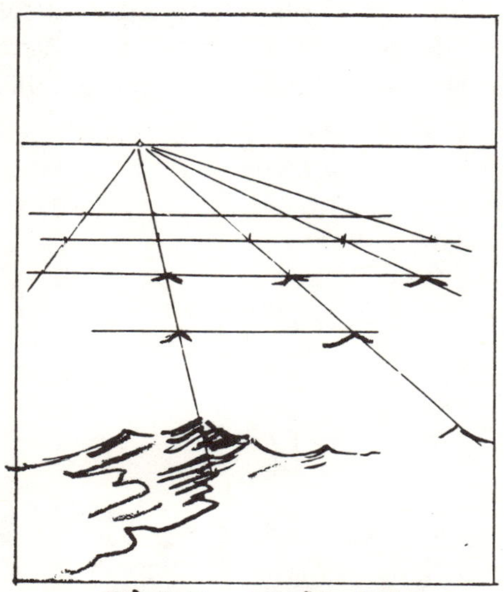

ONE WAVE

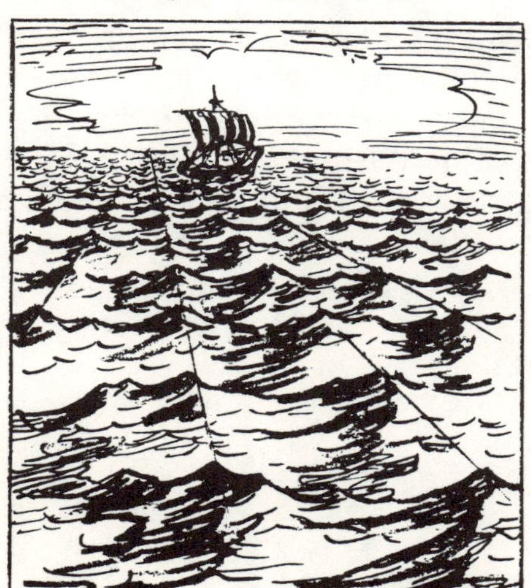

MORE WAVES

HEIGHTS OF PEOPLE NEAR AND FAR

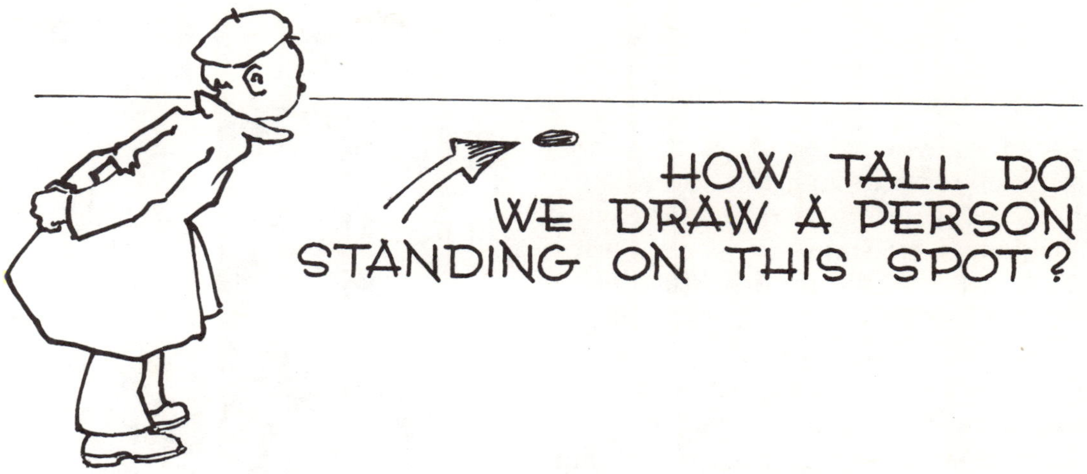

HOW TALL DO WE DRAW A PERSON STANDING ON THIS SPOT?

FIRST — A LINE THROUGH THE SPOT TO THE HORIZON. WE START THE LINE AT THE MAN'S FEET.

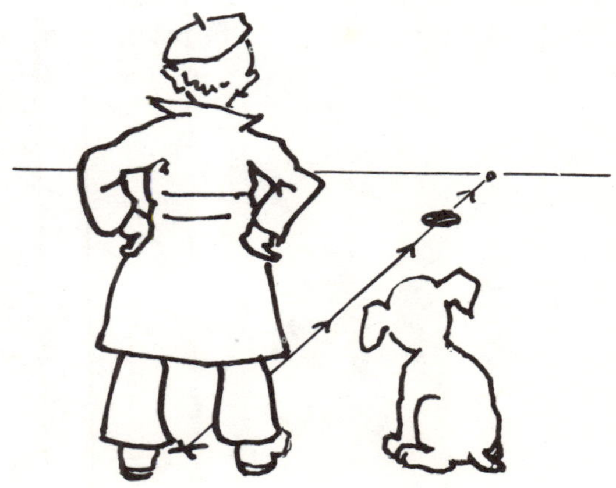

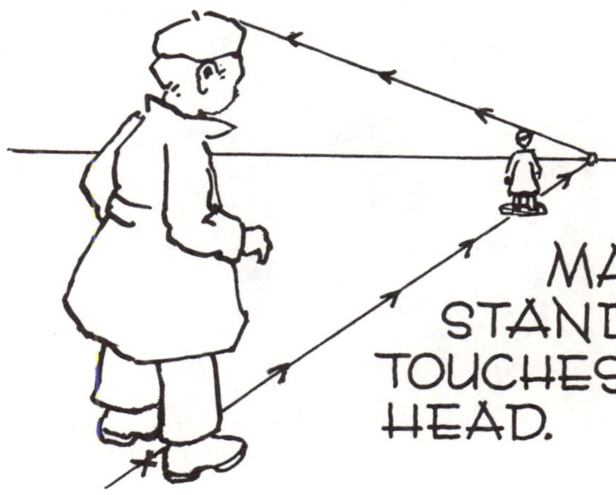

NEXT — FROM THE POINT ON THE HORIZON DRAW THE LINE BACK TO THE MAN'S HEAD. A MAN STANDING ON THE SPOT TOUCHES THIS LINE WITH HIS HEAD.

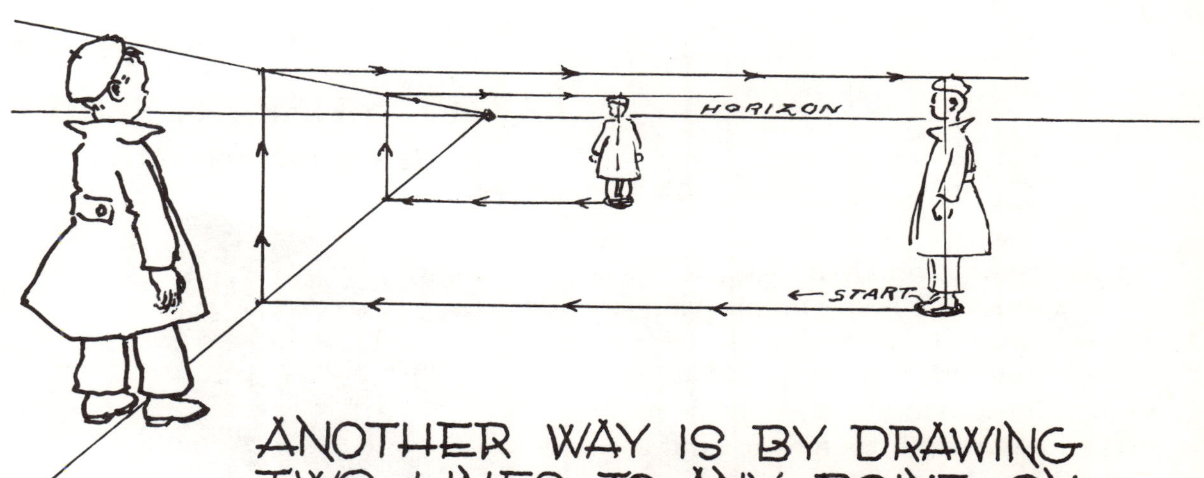

ANOTHER WAY IS BY DRAWING TWO LINES TO ANY POINT ON THE HORIZON. THEN START FROM THE SPOT AND DRAW THE HORIZONTAL AND PERPENDICULAR LINES SHOWN BY ARROW.

More Ways To Learn...With Walter Foster!

BEGINNERS ART SERIES
Introductory Art Skills

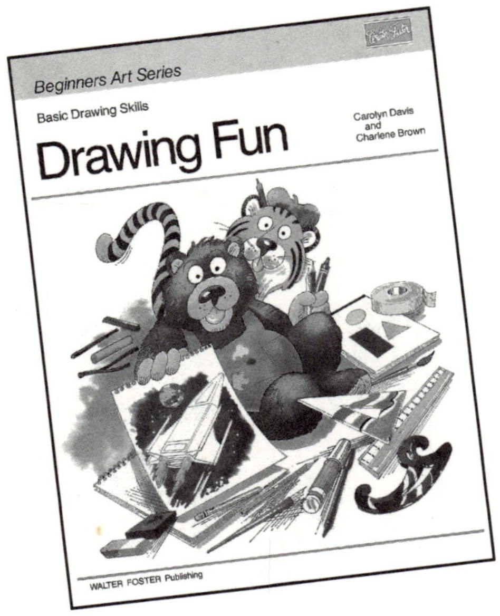

Looking for a way to spend "quality time" with the children in your life? Introduce them to the wonderful world of art...with the **Beginners Art Series** by Walter Foster Publishing. For $5.95 per title, this innovative instructional series teaches them the basics of art and art theory...expands their creativity...and develops their tactile and visual skills. Children ages six and up will be enthralled for hours...whether it's *Drawing Fun, Color Fun, Clay Fun, Comic Strip Fun, Poster/Lettering Fun, Paper Art Fun*...or all six titles. Written by experts in art education, these books provide demonstrations with easy-to-understand instructions and follow a standardized format including: a glossary of art vocabulary, a section on materials listing the tools associated with each topic, and a series of exciting projects for "hands on" creative experience.

HOW TO SERIES
Developing Art Skills

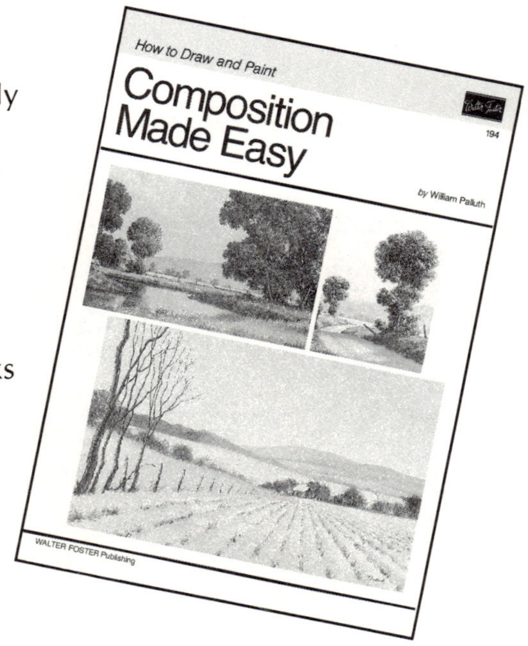

Now you can develop your art skills...easily and economically! The **How To Series** shows you how with art books addressing all media—pencil, watercolor, oil, acrylic, pen & ink, charcoal and pastel...and a variety of subject matter—animals, cartoons, figures, landscapes, seascapes, still life and more.

Written by accomplished artists, the books in the **How To Series** will help you improve your skills to become the best artist you can be! You will enjoy exploring the basics of form, line and dimension ...and learn the intricacies of advanced rendering techniques. You'll learn secrets that have helped our authors achieve excellence in their artistic specialties. There are over 100 titles in the Walter Foster **How To Series.** At only $3.95 per title these books fit every budget!

ARTIST'S LIBRARY SERIES
Advanced Art Skills

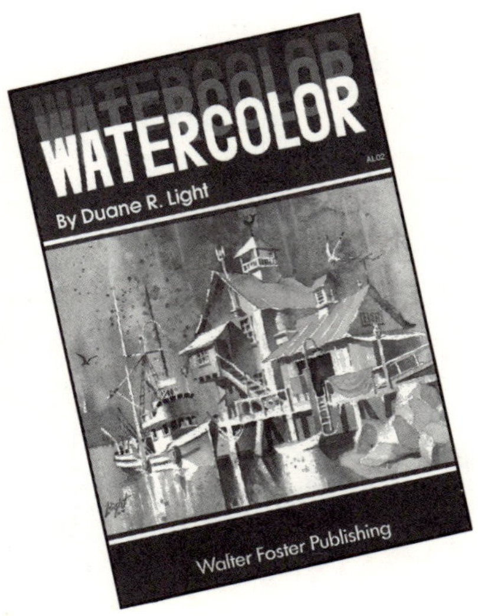

If you're serious about art, you don't want to be without the books in the Walter Foster **Artist's Library Series.** Focusing on a specific medium, subject or technique, each of these books teaches you complete procedures, from beginning to end.

The **Artist's Library Series** offers books addressing oil painting, watercolors, pencil drawing, acrylics, color theory, pen & ink, colored pencils, pastels, airbrush, calligraphy, impressionism, dry-brush watercolor, perspective and cartooning. You will find that these books are invaluable reference guides...No other texts offer such unique instruction at such a reasonable price—only $5.95 per title. The **Artist's Library Series** is sure to be a welcome addition to your library of art books!

Walter Foster Publishing ... The most recognized name in art publishing for more than 73 years.